Stepping Outside
Your Comfort Zone

Stepping Outside Your Comfort Zone

Lessons for School Leaders

Nelson Beaudoin

EYE ON EDUCATION
6 DEPOT WAY WEST, SUITE 106
LARCHMONT, NY 10538
(914) 833-0551
(914) 833-0761 fax
www.eyeoneducation.com

Library of Congress Cataloging-in-Publication Data

Beaudoin, Nelson.
    Stepping outside your comfort zone : lessons for school leaders / Nelson
    Beaudoin.
        p. cm.
    ISBN 1-930556-94-2
    1. School principals—United States—Anecdotes. 2. Educational
    leadership—United States—Anecdotes. I. Title.
    LB2831.92.B43 2005
    371.2'011—dc22

                                                                                    2004021265

Editorial services and production provided by
UB Communications, 10 Lodge Lane, Parsippany, NJ 07054
(973) 331-9391

Also available from Eye On Education

What Great Principals Do *Differently*:
15 Things That Matter Most
Todd Whitaker

What Great Teachers Do *Differently*:
14 Things That Matter Most
Todd Whitaker

Six Types of Teachers
Recruiting, Retaining, and Mentoring the Best
Douglas J. Fiore and Todd Whitaker

BRAVO Principal!
Sandra Harris

Dealing with Difficult Teachers, Second Edition
Todd Whitaker

Motivating & Inspiring Teachers
The Educational Leader's Guide for Building Staff Morale
Todd Whitaker, Beth Whitaker, and Dale Lumpa

Dealing with Difficult Parents
(And with Parents in Difficult Situations)
Todd Whitaker and Douglas Fiore

The Principal as Instructional Leader:
A Handbook for Supervisors
Sally J. Zepeda

Instructional Leadership for School Improvement
Sally J. Zepeda

Supervision Across the Content Areas
Sally J. Zepeda and R. Stewart Mayers

Standards of Practice for Teachers:
A Brief Handbook
P. Diane Frey, Mary Jane Smart, and Sue A. Walker

Harnessing the Power of Resistance:
A Guide for Educators
Jared Scherz

Achievement Now!
How to Assure No Child Is Left Behind
Dr. Donald J. Fielder

The ISLLC Standards in Action:
A Principal's Handbook
Carol Engler

Teaching Matters:
Motivating & Inspiring Yourself
Todd and Beth Whitaker

101 Answers for New Teachers and Their Mentors:
Effective Teaching Tips for Daily Classroom Use
Annette L. Breaux

Data Analysis for Continuous School Improvement
Victoria L. Bernhardt

School Leader Internship: Developing, Monitoring,
and Evaluating Your Leadership Experience
Gary Martin, William Wright, and Arnold Danzig

Handbook on Teacher Evaluation:
Assessing & Improving Performance
James Stronge & Pamela Tucker

Handbook on Educational Specialist Evaluation:
Assessing & Improving Performance
James Stronge & Pamela Tucker

Handbook on Teacher Portfolios
for Evaluation and Professional Development
Pamela Tucker & James Stronge

Beyond Measure: Neglected Elements of
Accountability in Schools
Edited by Patricia E. Holland

Dedication

To my wife Sharon
for her constant support,
and to Jamie and Matthew
who continue to enrich our lives.

Meet the Author

With over thirty-four years of experience in educational leadership, Nelson Beaudoin brings practical and exciting ideas to the discussion on school reform. His work is guided by the belief that leaders should listen more than talk, care more than judge, and understand more than guess.

Beaudoin has led two high schools through a Comprehensive School Reform grant. His schools have received national recognition both as a Service Learning Leader School (2001) and as a First Amendment Project School (2004). He was selected Maine's 2000 NASSP Principal of the Year.

He has presented his message about inspirational leadership, the magic of student voice, and creating a culture of change throughout the country. His faculty's work on Professional Learning Communities, Student-Led Conferences, and Student Engagement has been replicated in a number of schools.

Nelson Beaudoin is currently principal at Kennebunk High School in Kennebunk, Maine.

Table of Contents

Preface

Several astounding events led to the development of this book. The first was receiving a communication from a publisher asking me to put my stories in writing. He had heard me present at a conference, enjoyed my storytelling, and felt that my stories would provide meaningful lessons for other school leaders.

I am in my thirty-fourth year as an educator, and my focus has always been on the school and students I serve. Never had I considered branching out to a wider audience. This invitation to write my stories hit a nerve of wonderment, so I decided to pursue it further. After numerous conversations with the publisher, I attempted to write down some of my stories. Amazingly, this was easier than I had thought it would be. When I started writing, I realized that I had many stories to tell. With each story that I completed, another idea popped into my head. Soon I had completed a dozen stories. These stories seemed to have meaning—and bring enjoyment—to friends and colleagues with whom I shared drafts. I was still not convinced though that I was writing a book. I was at a loss regarding a central focus that would tie the stories together.

One weekend when my youngest son, Matt, came home for a visit, I decided to share my first dozen stories with him. I had paid a lot of money for his four-year degree in English literature, so why not get his critique? Matt had witnessed my work first hand. He had spent his youth attending schools where I worked. He had also worked on my faculty as a long-term substitute teacher. After he read my stories and we talked about them, I mentioned that I had a hard time believing that this work would ever reach publication. I couldn't see how all these stories would connect to one another.

My son awoke the next morning and told me that he had thought of a focus for my book. He suggested that I write about experiences that demonstrate my willingness to take risks. He recollected that most of my work involved my leaving my comfort zone. He went on to give me a few examples of what he meant. As I listened, I started to agree that the notion of stepping outside one's comfort zone had some merit. I have always sensed that great things usually don't happen to those who are cautious and guarded. Great things happen in a climate of exploration and risk. Matt was right—whether I was a teacher, coach, or administrator, I often operated outside my comfort zone.

Leading from outside, or even within the fringes, of one's comfort zone is somewhat of a rarity in schools nowadays. Educators typically choose familiarity and safety when faced with making decisions. Considering the pressures and demands they encounter, the reluctance to experiment is understandable. Predictable results and the avoidance of controversy seem more compelling than the unknown consequences of new ideas. The notion of passing my decisions through a filter that is not focused on control and predictability frees me to consider what is best for students. This route may lead to high levels of anxiety and tension, but it also leads to excitement and inspiration. In considering this concept, I realized that I had found the foundation for most of my stories. This awakening was the second extraordinary event that occurred as this book was unfolding. My son had determined the purpose of this work. He had identified a compelling reason that someone might have for reading this collection of stories.

The book evolved naturally into four sections. Each section has a special meaning and serves to link the stories together. "Making a Difference," "Images of Leadership," "Giving Students Voice," and "Educational Change" could comfortably apply to any of the accounts found in this book. Between the lines of each narrative, you will sense my effort to make a difference for my school and its students. This commitment allows me to approach my work as an educator with the courage to do things differently. Maintaining the status quo or taking the most comfortable route does not often create the necessary stimulus for different outcomes to occur in classrooms. The desired results of improving schools are more likely to transpire in a climate of innovation. The stories within this book illustrate how taking risks can result in positive changes.

I could never write or speak about my occupation without addressing the role of students as partners in my journey. The value of student voice and the exceptional accomplishments that I have observed because of it cannot be overstated. Students keep me both grounded and suspended through it all.

As I expand on the notion of leaving one's comfort zone, the idea of change threads its way through each story. Change leads to discomfort, to feelings of incompetence and self-doubt. But even though those feelings exist, I hope to show that the outcomes are usually good and sometimes miraculous. My students, my staff, and I have been the beneficiaries each time I have explored the world beyond my comfort zone.

The prospect that these simple stories may have meaning and influence others has helped me to overcome my initial reluctance to write and led me to venture into an area of what I consider risk. In many ways, this work plays back on itself. I have written it from a familiar place—outside my comfort zone. Perhaps this book will demonstrate that it is from there that good things tend to happen.

1

Making a Difference

Beacons of Hope

Don't Underestimate the Potential
Influence of Educators

It is easy for me to view young people as carriers of great potential. While society seems bent on keeping score and ranking people from good to bad, I follow a different path. Everyone is a masterpiece in the making. I came about this philosophy as a result of my own experiences. The following story illustrates how I went from the bottom of the heap to a position of leadership. It is not your typical rags to riches tale. I am certainly not rich—nor did I start out in rags. It is, however, a story about my academic awakening that leaves me hopeful as we strive to encourage each student to succeed and try to make a difference in each student's life.

I grew up in a bilingual family in which French was spoken at home. My early recollections of schooling are flooded with memories of confusion and struggle. I was stuck between two cultures and two languages. I was not a whole person in either area. Kids my age played little league baseball while I traveled to Franco-American events. Kids my age had a language they were confident in using and with which they could express their personality. I was suspended between two worlds and could not really express myself in either. Back in the 1950s, kids like me were trapped by the desire to be Americanized while parents were attempting to keep their foreign customs intact.

I often see students give up on academic work because of their fear of failure. I had done that very thing in elementary school. It was easier to not try than it was to expose my weaknesses. In particular, I remember shutting down in language arts. That subject was always so confusing to me. I thought in French, but had to speak and write in English. As a result, my grades were mediocre at best.

Once I entered high school I was tracked in standard classes. Teachers had low demands, and I delivered what was expected. My report cards were dominated by Ds and Cs. Occasionally I would stumble across a teacher I liked and would squeeze out a

B. I spent my school hours anticipating basketball practice and avoiding exposing my academic deficiencies. Luckily, though, I was not a huge behavior problem. My one trip to the principal's office occurred when I kidded a teacher in a history class about being a war baby. As she explained the term, I remarked that she must have been a Revolutionary War baby. Neither she nor the principal appreciated my sense of humor.

My school experience followed a fairly uneventful path. I put forth mediocre effort, received mediocre results, and comforted myself with low aspirations. Several events occurred that allowed this pattern to crack and finally break. The first occurred in basketball when an adult recognized me in a positive way. I had been cut from the eighth grade basketball team in favor of several athletic sixth graders. After one of these boys was injured, the coach asked me to fill in. You have no way of knowing how bad I was at basketball, but here's a little insight: I had scored a basket in an intramural game that the coach was watching. This was the only basket I had ever scored in an official game. I played about nine games with the eighth grade team after being added to the roster, and I never came close to scoring another basket. Two years later, in a junior varsity game, I scored ten points and was called to a meeting involving my coach and the varsity coach. They praised me for the improvement I had shown over the past two years and were obviously happy to have me in the program.

Although I did not become an All-American player—not even close—I did go on to enroll in college so that I could continue playing basketball. My career goal was to become a coach, because those two coaches who had given me the time of day were my heroes. They fueled my motivation for the game, and I wanted to be just like them. They had made a difference for me. How many students walk through the halls of our schools without ever being noticed? I was indeed one of the lucky ones.

My academic awakening came a little later. In fact, my growth in this area was incremental and continues to this day. During my junior year my family moved to a new community, and I transferred to a different high school. By some twist of fate or scheduling mix-up, I was placed in an Honors English class. As you probably remember, language arts was a struggle for me even in the general track. Here I was, a new kid in town, placed in an English class with the brainiacs. The English teacher knew I had limited skills—the red ink on my returned papers proved that. Yet on most of my papers he wrote positive comments about my ideas. I would earn an A for my thoughts and an F for my writing, averaging out to a C. I found this class interesting and worked hard to keep up with my new class-mates. By the end of the year I was doing B work and occasionally mustered up the courage to participate in class discussions. This teacher believed in me, just as my coaches had before him. I respected him and in turn wanted to deliver what he expected of me.

A year later, when I was participating in graduation, I was solidly in the bottom third of my class, so I certainly wasn't expecting any awards. Yet I received a National Commended Scholars Award, which was based on my performance on the PSAT test. The honor was not a result of my verbal score, but I had done well in the math section. Apparently I had some ability after all; I had just become conditioned to think otherwise or at least to keep it hidden.

My academic life has been a series of these small discoveries, each providing me with more confidence. A less than stellar college transcript revealed some isolated A's. They happened to be in the toughest courses because they were taught by a professor who thought I was his best student. I made sure not to disappoint him. I also was given an extremely difficult student teaching assignment because my supervising teacher felt I could rise to the occasion. I didn't disappoint her either.

All of these situations included a similar scenario. Someone expected more from me than I expected from myself. The teachers believed in me and gave me the courage to take a risk. Our schools are filled with youngsters who should be provided with challenges. They need to believe that they can achieve and receive the support to do it. Teachers can be much more than transmitters of information—they can be transmitters of hope. One caring teacher or coach can become a beacon of hope for a student who would otherwise go through school without success. I was fortunate enough to have several of them. Since entering the educational profession, I have worked to be that beacon for others.

My academic and personal transformations have continued through each decade of my life. In my twenties I came to believe I could be a leader on our faculty. In my thirties I started to confront my verbal weaknesses. I began writing and speaking with more confidence. My forties led to my belief that I could manage a school well, and I thus became a principal. And now in my fifties I have been encouraged to put my experiences in writing. Each of these progressions has been influenced by other people—the many beacons in my life who unknowingly guided me outside my comfort zone.

A Haircut and an Oil Change

Our Words and Actions Can Have a Profound Influence

One Monday, I was rushing out of my office on my way to some mission in another part of the school. As I got to the end of the long hallway leading out of the main office area, I realized that I had mindlessly walked past the receptionist's area without saying good morning to our wonderful secretary. I turned and wished her a good morning, and she replied, "Good morning Mr. Beaudoin. You had your oil changed this weekend, didn't you?"

This question stopped me in my tracks. I indeed had had my oil changed on Saturday, but how did she know? I glanced down at my fingernails to see if perhaps they were revealing oil stains and walked back to her desk to find out where she had gotten this information.

I asked her how she knew that I had had my oil changed. Had she been in my community on Saturday? I live an hour away from school, so that was unlikely.

She replied, "Of course not. I just know these things. There is not much you can do without my knowing it."

After a long pause and giggle, she decided to end my confusion by saying, "My daughter told me once that you always get your oil changed on the same day that you get a haircut. I noticed your nice haircut, so it stands to reason that you got your oil changed too."

It seems that after a snow day several years before, her daughter, who graduated last June, had complimented me on my haircut. I had made some foolish response like "I love snow days. I get to do all the things that are long overdue. I not only went to the barbershop; I also got my oil changed."

The receptionist and I had a great chuckle that morning. As I walked away, my mind started racing. How did this subject ever come up in their family conversation? Knowing this student well, I pictured the daughter insisting to her mother that because she had a hair appointment, she absolutely had to have her oil changed too! I can see her laughing as she qualified the idea to her puzzled mother—by simply stating that is what her principal does.

This story shows the untold influences we have on the students we serve. If my receptionist's daughter remembered my comments about a haircut and an oil change enough to repeat them at the dinner table, what else does she remember? How often does what I say get talked about at family gatherings? Did I ever make a comment to her about ethical choices, about how to treat others, or how to work through the peaks and valleys of daily life? My hunch is that there is something in her memory bank about me that has more relevance than an oil change. As educators, we can have profound influence on students. On occasion, we are fortunate enough to find out what a difference we made, but more often than not what we contribute goes undetected. We can only hope that we use this gift of influence wisely. As educators, we must remember the potential significance of our words and actions.

I Love This Job

Choosing a Positive Attitude Is Not Easy—
You Have to Work at It

After a regional track meet ten years ago, I was invited to a gathering at the home of a coach who lived in a community where I used to work. At the party, I bumped into many old friends and was able to share what I was currently doing and to find out where the years had taken them. Among those with whom I struck up conversations, one in particular stays with me to this day.

I ran into an old colleague who had coached for me years earlier. When he asked how things were going in my new job, I responded with a rolling of the eyes and a sarcastic remark, "It's going." His comment, upon hearing my reply, went something like this: "Gosh, Nelson, are you ever going to be satisfied in your work? Every time I talk to you, you're lamenting about how difficult and challenging your position is." At the time I did not give much thought to his comment other than to clarify that I really did not hate my job as much as I might have implied.

Today I look back on that simple conversation and see much more meaning than I did back then. Now, when an old acquaintance asks me how things are going, my answer is usually much more upbeat. I say that I am really having fun or that I am still enjoying my school and great things are happening.

What has happened to me over the past decade that has changed how I speak about my work? Am I more successful, am I more committed to what I am doing, am I confronted with fewer problems, or has my outlook changed?

I believe that in all of my positions in education I have enjoyed a high degree of success. My wife and my family will tell you that I have always been committed to my work, perhaps to a fault. And, as societal pressures increase along with educational mandates, I am certainly not facing fewer problems. Without question, my outlook has changed!

A number of things may have contributed to this change in attitude. But ultimately, a change of job status was the key. I have moved to the position of principal, whereas ten years ago I was an assistant principal. Part of my frustration was that, as an assistant, I had all of the responsibility of running a school, but I had very little voice in the decision-making process. I worked hard and effectively, but I never really felt that I had much of a say in the programs I was overseeing. The frustration usually developed because I knew that if I were in charge, I would do things differently.

During all my years as an assistant I was the guy who did all the grunt work, which included the not-so-glamorous routine of monitoring discipline, attendance, and facilities management, as well as calling substitutes (boy, did I hate that). At best, this was repetitive work with little or no opportunity for seeing progress. There would always be discipline issues; students and teachers would always be absent. And if one leak in the roof was addressed, another would soon spring up.

I felt like a gerbil on a wheel. I was working hard but making seemingly little progress. This work was an everyday expectation, a foregone conclusion, and the opportunities for feeling like I was making a difference were limited. It was not that my work was not appreciated or that I didn't get my share of praise. It was, simply, that I was in a fairly routine position. I had difficulty perceiving that my efforts had much of an impact. All of this changed when I became a principal.

I remember an exercise that I participated in during the 2001 NASSP Principal of the Year convention in Washington, D.C. We were trying to address the projected shortage of school administrators and were asked to generate lists of the positive and negative aspects of our roles as school leaders. I had little difficulty generating a list of positives.

Of interest, my list was nearly the antithesis of the negatives listed above. The principalship provides you an incredible amount of responsibility and the voice to accompany it. It provides you with an endless variety of tasks, from ordinary to inventive. And, most important, the principalship affords one the possibility of making a difference, a difference that isn't isolated but instead is extremely public. There are opportunities to create feelings of optimism in others and, through that hope, to invoke change.

I love what I do, and I guess I always have. Looking back, I see that the work I did as a coach, a teacher, an athletic administrator, and an assistant principal offered many of the same opportunities, but I didn't recognize them. Part of my transformation from a somewhat cynical educator to one who exudes hope is probably the result of my feeling responsible for all of the other people in my organization. Without my realizing it, sitting in the leader's chair has allowed me to take risks, to venture outside my comfort zone, for the sake of my students, staff, and the community. I no longer have to accept the status quo that in the past had placed limits on my work or my imagination. Although my actions in previous positions may have been seen as somewhat "out of the box," I had not felt empowered to truly follow my own beliefs. My work had been restricted by perceived controls imposed by others, whereas in the role as principal I began to feel a greater freedom to follow my heart.

Today my assistants have to perform many of the same tasks that I once did. However, I hope that they view their work more positively because of my leadership, which includes an effort to empower others through shared decision making, encouraged innovation, and mutual trust.

I have always felt that an organization will eventually take on the personality of its leader. I set out every day to make a difference. By seeking to improve the quality of our programs and learning for our students, I create championship moments for others. This commitment leads to an ongoing cycle of positive reinforcement.

When I was an athletic administrator, I viewed the issuing of football equipment as a repetitive drudgery. It simply marked the beginning of yet another fall sports season. My hunch is that the coach saw this new season as an opportunity to start an undefeated campaign. He saw a new beginning, with little thought of seasons past.

As principal, I see the annual ninth grade orientation program as a new opportunity to reaffirm our commitment to great work. The feeling of ultimate responsibility helps me view things more positively—much like a coach. You really can choose your attitude, and as a principal, I have learned to polish that skill.

When I am introduced to someone as a high school principal, I typically receive words of sympathy. I work hard to dispel those perceptions because people should know that I have one of the greatest jobs going. Choosing the proper attitude about your work requires a concerted effort. I now put all of my effort into what is best for my students. The concerns about personal comfort, fear of failure, or encountering possible problems take a back seat to the more important question of student outcomes. In doing this, I sacrifice a little control, but I create opportunities to truly make a difference. Principals are in a unique position—they can positively affect the lives of nearly everyone in the school community. I love this job!

Missing My Exit
Recognizing Signs of Appreciation

When I accepted the position as principal at Kennebunk High School, I knew that I would have to face a long daily commute. During my first year I traveled about 80 minutes to and from work. I eventually moved a bit closer, but I still drive about 50 minutes each way. This distance was a huge challenge for me as I had always worked minutes away from home. I was accustomed to arriving at work early and completing most of my "To Do List" items before staff and students arrived. Now I was stuck in my car being uncharacteristically unproductive. Although I typically adapt to change quickly, this one was difficult.

In the early days I tried a variety of strategies to occupy my time during the long commute. Listening to books on tape, relaxing to music, or attempting—and failing—to use a dictaphone were all parts of my initial attempt at adjusting to this new reality. Following a month or two of experimentation, I recognized that none of these ideas were going to work for me. What did work was simply thinking of my day and doing some long range planning in my head. It turned out that this time for thought had a huge impact on my success at this new position, especially in the eyes of my students.

It was known throughout the school community that the new principal was driving a long distance to come to work every day. I had been in districts where a long commute had been perceived by the community as a real problem. Administrators need to be visible. They need to be involved in the life of the school. When the principal is seen as an outsider the community can be resentful. Fortunately, that did not happen to me.

In fact, the exact opposite happened. People acted as if I were making a huge sacrifice just to be with them. Many communications I had with students or parents started with an appreciative comment from them about the personal sacrifices I was making to help the school. They would start by saying either "Thank you so much for driving all this way each day," or "Please don't tire from the commute—we need you here." Rather than seeing my living situation as a negative, they viewed it as evidence of my commitment to the school. I suspect that this response is a truly unusual occurrence in education. I guess I am charmed.

One event in particular stands out as an example of how this commuting issue has been turned inside out for me. I arrived at school one day about fifteen minutes later than usual. I walked into a leadership team meeting apologizing for being late and giving an honest explanation about why. I had been driving down the turnpike thinking of initiatives that the school needed. I suddenly did not recognize the landscape along side of the road. My confusion ended when I realized that I had driven past my normal exit. I had been so deeply involved in thinking about school that I completely missed the exit.

Obviously this is not a wise practice. Admitting it to the leadership team probably should have raised concerns about my safety. To the contrary, however, my colleagues thought it was another example of my commitment to our school. One member of our leadership team, an eternal optimist, thought this was a story worth sharing with others. She told several students and parents. Word spread quickly throughout the community that I was so passionate about improving the school that I had actually driven past my exit. I was unaware that this story was percolating until a senior girl later ribbed me about missing my exit on the way to school. This is an amazing example of how the school community accepted my leadership and the distance issues that accompanied it.

At the conclusion of my second year at Kennebunk High School, the student body honored me by dedicating the yearbook to me. This was a special thrill for me, for I had never received such an award. As I listened to the student read the dedication during the commencement assembly, I was shocked to hear the mention of a missed exit. The dedication went as follows:

Mr. Beaudoin,

Last year you brought us Challenge Nites and Teen Issues Day, and we sensed a change in climate. This year we moved into the New York exchange, a sizable grant, and plans for more grants and more changes. You are tireless, and we really do appreciate how hard you try. We know that you think of us constantly and even, on occasion, miss the Kennebunk exit as plans for the future circulate through your head. You were even willing to "be suspended" during Spirit Week. Most of all, you listen to us, and no class, no student body, can ask for more than that.

The 2003 *Rambler* is dedicated to you as the smallest of tokens of our respect and gratitude.

I guess missing that exit was not so bad after all! It made me realize that students and staff really do appreciate me. I will think of ways to uphold that appreciation in future commutes.

A Voice From the Past

Opportunity for Growth Knocks
When You Least Expect It

It was 8:00 in the evening during mid-April 2003. I was sitting peaceably on the couch after a particularly taxing day. I did not want to move when I heard the phone ring, but I reached to take the call anyway.

"Hello," I said.

"Hello," responded a unfamiliar voice. "Would I be talking to Matt Beaudoin's father?"

"Yes, I am Matt's dad."

A weird feeling of panic rushed over me. Had something bad happened to our son who worked in Boston? I did not like the initial tone of this phone call.

"Oh good!" replied the caller. "Then I must have the right Nelson Beaudoin. You probably don't remember me, but this is Jake Edwards."*

"Oh my gosh, Jake Edwards! How are you doing?"

* * *

I certainly did remember Jake. He had played basketball for me twenty-five years earlier. I remember nearly all of my players from the past. Coaching creates such a strong interpersonal bond between the coach and student athletes. My mind's eye can still visualize most of the players. But this was Jake Edwards, one of the players that I would be least likely to forget.

I remember going to a well-respected college coach to seek advice about Jake. Jake was a talented eighth grader who had the potential to be the best high school player I ever coached. The question that I had for my mentor revolved around my fear that I would not be able to keep Jake in my program. He had great physical skills but had displayed difficulty controlling his temper in competitive situations. I questioned whether Jake would be able to adhere to my strict rule about not incurring

---

*Name has been changed.

technical fouls. In nearly every game I had seen him play, he had self-destructed emotionally. In my mind I knew that this behavior would continue in high school and that I eventually would have to ask him to leave the program.

The coach gave me some simple, but surprising, advice: "Sounds like you need to change your rules!" He went on to say that Jake was a special talent with a strong competitive spirit. He warned me about the danger of breaking that spirit with absolute rules. He advised me to work toward the goal of self-control with Jake in smaller increments. This strategy would allow him to grow through his mistakes and eventually become a player I could count on. The coach's advice was somewhat shocking. He was suggesting that I alter a long-standing rule that I felt strongly about. He was also suggesting that I could help Jake over time, when what I really wanted was a quick fix. It was obvious that I would have to leave my comfort zone in order to help this student.

During the three years that Jake played on the varsity team he never drew a technical foul. He teetered on the edge on a number of occasions, but I followed my mentor's advice and worked toward continual improvement. The plan worked well. Jake became a solid, consistent player. My coaching mentor had taught me a valuable lesson about being flexible. That trait is essential as I strive to make a difference for each student.

*   *   *

The phone conversation with Jake continued.

"I am doing pretty good," he answered. "I have three kids, a good job, and live in Freeport."

"That is great," I said.

"I was thinking about you the other day as I found this letter you had written me. I thought I should try to look you up."

I responded that I was thrilled he had called and suggested that because we lived within an hour of each other, perhaps we could get together sometime. I took his phone number, and then I asked about the letter he had stumbled across.

"Yeah, I found it when going through some stuff the other day, and I thought I should give you a call," he replied.

"It is amazing that you still have it," I responded. "I still occasionally write long letters like that to students or teachers. What was the letter about?"

Jake paused to think for a minute, then answered, "Oh pretty much that I was a rear end, but you need to know I am doing okay now."

We talked for another ten minutes or so, exchanging news about our families and our lives. When my wife got home I told her about my surprise phone call and how great Jake sounded. I reminded her that he was in his forties now. My how time flies. I couldn't help but feel that I was still influencing this student to a small degree even though twenty-five years had passed.

For the rest of that evening I reflected on that letter I had written to Jake. In the interest of making a difference for students, I have written fifteen or twenty such letters over the years. I wrote them as a result of becoming invested in a student or situation. These letters probably symbolize carrying my passion a bit too far. I often wonder if the time, energy, and investment paid any dividends over time. This particular letter still seemed to have meaning twenty-five years after it was delivered.

I knew that Jake's letter had been written at a time when he was out with an injury. I also remembered that it was written in part to explain my rationale for not selecting him as team captain. I was quite certain that it must have included some sermon regarding his temper. I wondered if the letter honored Jake or if he was a victim of my adult "know it all" attitude.

In spite of my apprehension about Jake's letter and how good or bad it was, I felt really good about his phone call. He had been a huge part of my life back then. The call made me realize that I must have made a difference in his life. I know that this was my motivation for writing the letter in the first place. Sometimes, in education it takes a while to see one's efforts pay off. I am equally certain that I grew from this experience as well. Sometimes it is through giving that we receive.

Perhaps now that Jake and I have reconnected, our personal growth may continue. I fully intend to give Jake a call and meet with him. Maybe he will show me the letter so I can learn from this experience. Making a difference is rarely a one-way street.

Championship Moments

The Smallest of Gestures Can Make the Biggest Difference

Much of my work in education is aimed at accumulating championship moments, yet what one expects at the height of such occasions has rarely happened to me. Only two instances come to mind: I was once carried off the basketball court after making a buzzer beater from forty feet to win a game. Another time, I rolled twelve consecutive strikes to record the only perfect game ever bowled at Jerry-Brook Lanes in Augusta, Maine. Both of these are fond memories for me. Granted, the win for my college basketball team was our first in eight games, and perfection in the sport of bowling has eluded me for the past seventeen years. (Of interest, the owners of Jerry-Brook Lanes decided that my accomplishment should be rewarded with lifetime free bowling. The establishment closed eight months later.) These two exceptions to my otherwise ordinary athletic skills probably say more about luck than innate ability.

The championship moments that punctuate my work life are completely different. I am not the primary benefactor; luck has nothing to do with it; and the moments, rather than being rarities, seem to grow geometrically. Given that I see the work of a principal as more of a ministry than a job, my memories of my profession are absolutely cluttered with championship moments. I offer here a few examples, which are intended to give you a hint about these wonderful interactions and the lessons I learned from them.

* * *

It is extremely difficult to tell a student (and his parents) that he is no longer permitted in school because of a mistake that he made. A while back, I had the misfortune of having a student leave school three months prior to graduation because of repeated infractions of our substance abuse policy. Rather than go through a formal expulsion hearing, we came to an agreement that would allow the student to get his diploma in a private ceremony. He had to complete his requirements through a home tutorial and attend counseling. The student and the parent agreed, but I could tell that the door being closed to participating in our commencement was a devastating blow. Despite the intense emotions concerning the graduation ceremony, I held my ground, and we entered into a verbal contract.

One week before graduation the student called and asked to meet with me. Upon his arrival at my office I knew what this meeting was about. The struggling teen who had left school, at my request, eight weeks earlier no longer existed. He had been replaced by a polite, sober, and engaging young adult who wanted to participate in graduation for his family's sake. He had been attending counseling with obvious success, had been straight since the incident, had completed all his work at an exemplary level, and wanted so much to make his past a fading memory. I had every reason to deny his request. In fact, public sentiment probably leaned toward my saying no. After all, the school had already struck a deal that was more than generous. The student could have been expelled. But by granting participation in graduation, I provided this student and his family a championship moment. My assistant principal framed this decision perfectly when he said, "What are we all about, if it is not to get students to finally succeed?"

* * *

I was sitting in my office at a table working on the budget when I glanced up and saw two senior girls signing out for early release. I looked up and said quite loudly, "Now there are two reasons why I love my job!" The girls looked startled at first, then glanced at each other and giggled. One of them said, "Oh, that is so nice."

A few weeks earlier, these girls had given up two days of school vacation to be trained as mediators for a peer mediation program that we were developing. They had already successfully mediated a conflict between two groups of ninth grade girls, and as such they had kicked off our new program in fine fashion.

I'm not sure that they made the connection between my statement that they were the reason I loved my job and their work as peer mediators. That really didn't matter. What mattered was that they understood that I really valued them. A kind word, a compliment, or an off-the-cuff comment can create a championship moment for anyone.

*   *   *

The new superintendent in our district volunteered to teach a drug awareness/leadership course at my school. He has a wealth of knowledge on the subject and is a charismatic speaker. The course has been a huge success. The students truly look forward to this class. The fifteen students involved meet with him during their thirty-minute lunch period. As the first semester ended, one of the students discovered that her lunch period would change because of her second semester class schedule. She was devastated that she would have to give up this special course. She thoughtfully e-mailed the superintendent with her apology.

The superintendent asked me if I could do anything to change the schedule so that this student's class would eat at a time that would allow her to continue with the program. I did not even have to think about whether I would do this—a championship moment was at stake.

I spent the better part of a morning trying to shuffle classes between "A" and "C" lunch with no success. Every switch I investigated put another student in a bad position. I could have felt put out that I was putting forth so much energy for one student just for a noncredit course. But it mattered a great deal to her, and I needed to make it happen. I finally succeeded, thanks to the flexibility of the student's teacher, who agreed to release her from class to attend the superintendent's special course.

When I broke the news to the student she seemed almost embarrassed that we had gone to all this trouble. I asked her how important this special class was to her. She replied that "it was awesome" and that she would "love to continue, but . . . ." I interrupted her, ending the conversation with " 'Nough said." This student completed the course and became a strong proponent of the program. Schools need to go the extra mile to support the passion of students.

*　*　*

There are a variety of ways to acknowledge and encourage staff members' efforts. I believe that one way to improve a school is to make your great teachers better. This raises the bar for everyone. Consequently, I try to find small and not so small ways to recognize teacher accomplishments.

Before faculty meetings I have gone out and bought four or five $1 lottery tickets and presented some teachers with recognition cards and tickets for a job well done. Once one of our custodians won $500 off a $1 ticket. Staff members really enjoy the recognition.

At the end of each summer recess I take the custodial staff out for breakfast. This is my way of thanking them for all that they have done to prepare for the opening of school. It is also an opportunity for me to tell them that although they may see very little of me in the next five or six months, they need to recognize how vital they are to our school's success.

I frequently write notes to my superintendent about different employees who have done something above and beyond their duties. I often mention that one person or another is a treasure. The superintendent usually shares this information with the school board during a public meeting.

After having made such a big deal about trying to reach our goal of 100% participation in student-led conferences (see page 51), I needed to find a way to honor our accomplishments. We set up a yard-sale type of table at a faculty meeting stocked with inexpensive novelty gifts. Any faculty member who had achieved our target goal by having all of his or her advisees participate in conferences was invited to select a gift in honor of the accomplishment.

In order to inspire people to work toward high standards, one must be willing to recognize and honor their efforts.

*　*　*

Several years ago I had a meeting with a student who had established a strong pattern of failure. This student had yet to earn a credit, and he was now in his third year of high school! He was actually attending our alternative school and this was an intervention aimed at removing him from the roster to create room for a student who would be willing to make progress. The student was under contract that required earning credit or relinquishing his spot in our alternative program. The standard format for this type of meeting would be to lay out the facts and cut the student loose. We instead tried to paint the picture in a positive light. We offered the student a sabbatical leave from high school and setting up an internship with a local cabinet maker. We made it clear that following this experience, if the student was willing to return to classes, he would be welcomed back. In this case it worked. The student returned to school the following semester and started to experience school success.

* * *

Some championship moments backfire. One year I spent the better part of a summer with a student producing a tremendous video production on school reform to show on the first day of school. We included memorable movie clips from the best-known Hollywood films about education, great graphics, hip music, and subtle messages about school change. The production ended with a skit modeled after Chris Farley's Saturday Night Live character Matt Foley.

I was so proud of the production that I approached the leadership team with the idea of having all of our students enter the gymnasium on the first day of school and, with no introduction, just view the video. They agreed.

The idea absolutely bombed! The students were so hyper returning back to school that they had trouble focusing. The presentation, which was crystal clear to me, missed the mark with most students. It would have been fine had we done some thoughtful introduction or shown it later in the day, but the damage had been done. A championship moment had been lost.

Even that failure turned out to be useful. Whenever I come up with a weird idea to present to the leadership team, I remind them to honestly tell me if I am off target. I indicate that I don't want them to simply go along as they did with the opening day video. We do the same with students, admitting that we blew that one, and they automatically pay more attention to the activity at hand.

* * *

All of these scenarios have a common thread. We are trying to create memorable events in the world of our students and staff. This thread ties closely with the notion of making a difference. We have within us the power to accomplish great things, or not so great things. We choose the former. We choose to make a difference.

Having Fun at Work

Let Your Humanity Show

The compelling goal of making a difference for others does not always take the form of compassion or thoughtfulness. Sometimes we can make a difference by bringing humor to a situation or by finding ways to divert people's attention away from the daily routine. I have often tried to bring humor into our faculty meetings because teachers are typically exhausted at these meetings and the meetings can be draining.

I spend a lot of time dreaming up funny skits or games just to change the routine. As much personnel time as this takes, I wish I could give this idea more attention. The silly ideas that are included here probably don't directly promote the mission of our school, but I believe they help create a climate where goals can be reached. When you work to create fun in the workplace, you sometimes have to risk giving up control. Letting go of the controls for the right reasons usually provides a great ending. The ending I am looking for is that our faculty and our students never lose their sense of humanity. We are on this planet to do more than work and learn—we are also here to laugh and enjoy. I have personally never had much of a problem in promoting the idea of having fun at work as the following examples illustrate.

* * *

While conducting my first faculty meeting at a new school, I selected as my first activity to do a spin-off of the TV show *Family Feud*. I had done a bit of research about our faculty over the summer and discovered funny tidbits about them. I created charts that replicated the television game board and called two teams of volunteers forward to play. I asked questions about "what the survey said" and either struck a gong for an incorrect answer or flipped the matching correct answer on the chart. The faculty chuckled cautiously at the beginning, started laughing as the idea that we were doing this settled in, and roared as the game came to an end. I had gotten them to move outside of their comfort zone and fully participate.

I had been told in my early conversations about this school that faculty meetings were dreaded affairs. I had taken the time to create a fun activity as the first order of business for the beginning of our work together. It proved to be a wise choice. Following the *Faculty Feud*, I asked my assistant principal to briefly review some minor changes in the student handbook. By the time he got to the second point, a real faculty feud started to occur. It was clear that this faculty member had to lighten up if we were going to change the perceptions of our meetings. I was glad that their first view of me was through a lens filtered by laughter. We certainly had a lot of work ahead of us to make fun a part of the school culture.

* * *

In trying to establish a culture of fun and laughter, I often become the subject of practical jokes. On one occasion I arrived at school several minutes late only to find a set of parents waiting to meet with me concerning their daughter. I walked them toward my office while apologizing for my tardiness. As I tried to open the door to allow the parents to enter, it would only open an inch or so. Peering in, I could see that someone had barricaded my door with every piece of furniture in the room. I quickly redirected the parents to the conference room, completed the meeting, and then began investigating what had happened to my work space.

Actually the case was easy to solve. There was only one person on staff who had the strength to move heavy desks and pick up file cabinets by himself. He was a science teacher and body builder whom I had been targeting at recent faculty meetings as the subject of some good-natured kidding. At the last faculty meeting, I had commented that he was fun to pick on because I knew he didn't have the courage to retaliate. I knew that eventually he would return my volley. He had come in early that morning, stockpiled everything I owned in front of my door, and climbed out the window. I doubt that he knew that I had an early morning meeting scheduled.

Word spread of my morning surprise, and smiles could be seen throughout the building. I never said a word to the teacher, but during second period he restored my office to its usual clutter.

I selected someone else at the next faculty meeting to joke with. The body builder had proved that I was no match for him.

* * *

I had introduced the idea of the FISH! philosophy at our opening-day workshop (see page 141). We had done several activities which revolved around the need to have fun, or play, at work. A month into the school year, I was standing in front of the faculty during our monthly meeting answering questions when I happened to call on a particular teacher. As soon as I said the teacher's name, a dozen faculty members stood and started singing the words to Arlo Guthrie's song "Alice's Restaurant." After singing several lines, very poorly, they all sprinted out the front door. They returned several minutes later through a side door, and we resumed the meeting.

I played it very cool and didn't react at all. To be honest, I had been tipped off that it was going to happen and that the idea was one faculty member's test to see whether I was serious about the FISH! idea of playing at work. The next morning I sent a memo asking faculty members if they knew the significance of why those dozen teachers were singing off key. I received some serious responses explaining that what had occurred was not to be taken personally, that it was just a going craze which had people leaving the business establishment and gathering on the street. Such events were called Raves.

I waited until several months had passed before I retaliated. I solicited the support of a dozen staff members, and we waited patiently for the faculty member who had organized the first rave to ask a question. When he finally did, my dozen volunteers and I began singing Don McLean's "American Pie" and walked out of the meeting.

The notion of play had gone full circle—unless the teacher wants to continue the game!

* * *

On several occasions I have had the opportunity to become a playwright. I have written several one-act plays involving seven or eight characters that have premiered at faculty meetings.

Basically, I come into a faculty meeting, select people to play the roles, and hand out scripts. The players halfheartedly perform their roles, and the audience gets a kick out of seeing their colleagues trying to act in these unrehearsed productions.

The real method to this madness comes in the content of the scripts. On one occasion, I introduced the idea of the educational shift toward standards and looked comically at the idea, and the fallacies, of politicians' raising the bar. Within the skit, I had the characters all achieve varying levels of success or failure relative to this imaginary standard. The idea effectively illustrated the point that these new standards were going to be a challenge. Doing it through humor probably helped make the message more digestible. I wrote another play to drive home the notion that we have students at our school who have to be exposed to other ways to win besides the four-year college path.

These ventures into theater are not in the least quality productions, but they do lead to quality faculty meetings. They break the monotony of straightforward, boring information and put a dose of reality into our deliberations.

*   *   *

When a member of my administrative team suggested that we start the school year by introducing ourselves to the faculty and describing our respective roles, I dreaded the idea. What could possibly be more boring? Yet I could see that what he was asking was important and needed. I ended up finding songs that represented each team member. My song was Roger Miller's "King of the Road;" another person's was Frank Sinatra's version of "I Did it My Way." I had two teachers, a novice and a veteran, guess who each song represented. Their answers and mistakes provided ample opportunities for laughs; the loud music was uplifting; and the faculty enjoyed the lighthearted way in which these introductions were approached. It took time to prepare, and time and to execute, but the outcome was all good.

*   *   *.

I used to love special days at elementary schools. Hat days were always my favorite, although I can't name my favorite hat—there have been so many! When the students saw me in a hat, or whatever else was the order of the day, their eyes would light up and add enjoyment to the event. Yes, principals can wear costumes on holidays. It is always good to take a step outside one's comfort zone and dare to show our humanity and sense of humor.

Leaving a Legacy

Believe in the Importance of Your Work
So That Your Work Becomes
Important to You

I think it was Stephen Covey, author of *Seven Habits of Highly Effective People*, who put the idea in my head that we should live, learn, love, and leave a legacy. As an educator, I can't imagine a better road map to follow. To keep a sense of optimism amidst difficult challenges, to hopefully learn as we go along so that our tomorrows are better than our yesterdays, and to love are great aspirations. And if they are done well, we just may leave a legacy. We just may make a difference.

In my thirty-four-plus years as an educator, I have had my share of ups and downs. This is at times a demanding, almost thankless, profession. As I look back at the work I have done to date, one thing makes me the proudest: I have had the privilege of hearing the music before the song is over! I am not sure that many educators have been this fortunate. The daily grind, the valleys of educational experiences, and the criticism that we are sometimes subjected to often blind us to our true accomplishments.

One of my teachers, upon retiring, shared with me a strategy that he had used during his long career to rise above the negativity. He had started a collection of positive notes and accomplishments that had come his way, and he revisited these whenever things seemed to start weighing on him. What a simple, but great idea! Upon hearing this, I decided to try this strategy. I only wish that I had found it earlier.

Dozens of years ago I was at my school on Memorial Day volunteering to open the school so that a group of students could rehearse for an upcoming play. While I was there, a school committee member showed up and asked me why the flag wasn't being flown on such an important national holiday. I am sure he had no ill intent by asking me this question, but it devastated me. I had given up a day with my family and a round of golf to serve our students, and this man could only criticize the fact that the flag wasn't flying. I surely could have used my collection of positive memories on that day.

The idea of hearing the music before the song is over should be a rallying cry for all educators. Most of us can look back on our careers and feel great pride in our accomplishments, but rarely do we take the time to celebrate them while they happen. Sometimes we don't even see them. That is why I can honestly say that I feel charmed. The old adage that success breeds success is applicable to the work of educators. If we can find ways to acknowledge our success, then greater success will follow.

I have dug out my collection of warm memories and want to share a few with you as I end this section on making a difference. Fittingly it is the first section of this book, because in the final analysis, this legacy is what our work is all about.

I will begin with two letters I received from students within a two-week period. What is interesting about these letters is that they came from two different schools from students with whom I had worked during different periods of my career. The fact that they both said essentially the same thing gave me a sense of accomplishment and a sense of consistency. These were both outstanding students who would have been outstanding even if I had never entered into the equation. The small part I played in their growth serves as an inspiration to me. Hopefully I can (and do) have the same type of influence on many students.

Mr. Beaudoin:

I want to thank you for *everything* this past school year. Looking back, your presence in the building had such a positive affect. You truly started a change in this school. Words cannot express how thankful I, and other students, are to have such an amazing principal. I also wanted to thank you for all the opportunities you have given me. You have inspired me and supported me, but most importantly you have empowered me and believed in what I can do. There is not enough room on this little card to thank you enough. It has truly been a pleasure to work with you, and I look forward to next year.

Junior Girl

Dear Mr. Beaudoin:

I never would have thought that the day in the gym (10th grade), when you asked me about service learning, would be such a pivotal day in my life. The impact it has had on my educational goals and me as a person is immeasurable. Also some of the friendships I have begun have been the best in my life.

You have also been in constant support of our service learning ventures. You have encouraged us, but ultimately gave us the responsibility of speaking. Your goals are for the students, not yourself. You are always giving for the benefit of others——you are a model to be emulated.

Thank you for having faith in me—you have made such a difference!

Senior Girl

Next are thoughtful comments I received from two other students who again are from two different schools. The first came on a card, and the second occurred in a passing conversation.

Mr. Beaudoin:

Over the last few years, you have helped to improve the learning environment at Leavitt. Your dedication to improving communication and learning here makes you a poster-child for secondary education. Thank you for the opportunities you have created for this school and its students.

Senior Boy

As I was passing a student in the hall, the following conversation with a senior girl ensued:

"Good morning Kim. How is it going?" I asked.

"Oh, Mr. Beaudoin, things are going just great. I am having such a great year."

"I'm glad to hear that."

"Well you should know that you are a big reason for my feeling this way. I used to hate school, but now I really look forward to it. The changes you have brought here are awesome."

"Thank you so much for those comments, but you know I had a lot of other people helping me, and you had to be willing to become involved."

"I know, Mr. Beaudoin, but I am still saying that you are the person who made all the difference, and I wanted you to know that."

I also have been fortunate enough to receive a tremendous amount of feedback from staff members. The fact that the following two notes came from veteran teachers makes them even more meaningful. Change is hard for everybody, but especially hard for people who have spent a number of years in one place. Both of these teachers are from Kennebunk High School. The tone of their notes indicates that this was a school that was ready for some changes.

Nelson:

Just a note before we head off for the holidays. Allow me to commend your first few months at K.H.S. In all my time here, no principal has had the kind of profound effect on staff and students that you have. The mood and atmosphere have changed for the better—to such a degree that it's difficult to remember our recent low point. People specifically mention you in the same breath when they talk about what is good about K.H.S. Your quiet nudging, your quick decisions, your ability to synthesize and report out, your gentle humor, and your genuine interest in students all have moved us to greener pastures.

I think one fear of teachers, parents, and students alike is that you may tire of the drive (or submit to the desire to see more of your wife) and be a one-year miracle. We need you here for more than that. The work has just begun. Again, on behalf on myself, and unofficially my department, thank you and happy holidays.

Veteran Teacher

Nelson:

Just a note to thank you for the magic you have brought to our school. For the first time in 25 years here I feel like we—teachers, students, and parents—are all on the "same page." The best Christmas present of all has been your presence here at Kennebunk High School.

Veteran Teacher

The next letter is a note from a former student who eventually became part of my faculty. At the time, he was leaving our school to take an administrative role in another district.

Nel:

I have never been particularly adept at asking for assistance and then giving thanks for it; yet you have always done anything for me without hesitation—I never know how to thank you. I always just hope you know what I think of you. Through it all you have shown such patience, provided support, been a voice of wisdom, and acted so cool under pressure. I've learned so much—countless things. Even when we are not in touch, I use the lessons you've taught. I am a better professional, a better person. Thanks for helping so much.

Former Student, Former Staff Member

The last example of things that allow me to see the influence I have involves a conversation I had with a parent several months ago. We were leaving the monthly principal/parent meeting and walking toward the parking lot. This mother was thanking me for taking the time to conduct these monthly meetings. She was extremely complimentary about the work we had done over the past several years. She went on to tell me that she had two students who graduated from this high school several years ago. They had not had a very good experience, but both were in college and doing fine. She had been concerned two years ago as her youngest was about to enter the school. She was so concerned that she stayed awake nights wishing she had the money to send her child to private school. With two other children in college, that wasn't about to happen.

On this night she made a point of telling me how pleased she was that she didn't opt for private school. Her child was absolutely loving high school, and she couldn't say enough about how much the school had changed from her vantage point. I encouraged her to e-mail our teachers and staff so that they would know how she felt.

All of these examples of positive comments that I've cited are not earth shattering. Most principals and most teachers have received similar compliments. They are included in this section because I believe that if you are open to the idea that your work is important, the more important it becomes.

We have to listen to the music above the background noise of our daily work to hear these affirmations that we do make a difference.

2

Images of Leadership

Stand for Something

Take Time to Create—and Live By— A Personal Motto

I often wish that I knew by name the man at the garage down the street. My constant moving from school to school has prohibited that from occurring. I will always wonder what it would have been like to spend forty years in one community and to have deeply established roots. Although I sometimes wonder what other turn my life could have taken, I have to acknowledge that my journey has been most satisfying.

We are all products of our experiences. I have been especially blessed to have worked in a number of different school systems. This has given me the advantage of observing several school leaders in various settings. Many people I have worked with do not have that vantage point. They have seen the schooling process from one perspective and have not had the luxury of multiple views.

I have always been an observer of people. For example, I would try to find the best qualities of the coaches I played for and blend them together to create my own best possible coaching style. My work in education has exposed me to more than a thousand different professionals. At least one hundred of them have been school leaders with whom I have worked closely. I believe that in some ways my work is a reflection of the strengths of many of these people. When considering the school principals with whom I have worked most closely, I know this is certainly the case. One was exceptionally cool under pressure and therefore a master at resolving conflict. Another was a strong leader who got others to rise to his expectations. Another principal was a visionary who created a dynamic culture of change within the school. Yet another was a people person who created a climate of trust and caring.

My hope as I began looking toward the principalship was to take these modeled characteristics and shape them into a style of my own. There were two things that I knew would be central to my leadership style. The first was the role of students. I have always connected well with students and have always known that they are the reason behind my work. As I aspired toward the position of principal I did not want that commitment to change. The second thing I was sure of was that I did not ever want to be seen in an adversary role. All of my previous experiences told me that I had much more in common with my students, fellow teachers, and parents than I had in contrast. I knew that my administrative skills would be more collaborative than authoritarian.

I remember sitting in my car awaiting my first interview for a principal's position. I had gotten to the interview site one-half hour early and was reviewing some answers I had written in preparation for anticipated interview questions. I have always used this strategy when preparing for interviews. Over the years I realized that if you have prepared some good answers, you will use them during the interview. The specific question for which you prepared a response may never be asked, but you will be able to insert the answer into a related question somewhere along the way.

As I read the answer I had prepared regarding my leadership style, I became a bit panicked. I had discussed participatory leadership and the fact that students are at the center of my work (both areas of strong belief), but I sensed that there was something missing.

I took out my pen and started jotting down some quick notes. I wrote down the word *caring* while thinking of one of the qualities of a past principal. Then I wrote down the word *knowledge* as a representation of the wealth of different experiences to which I had been exposed. Finally I wrote down the words *good listener*, a term reflecting the principal who had been so good at resolving conflict.

As I walked up to the stairs of the school, I restructured those words into a personal motto for school administration. I would seek to "listen more than I talk, care more than I judge, and understand more than I guess." I did not know it at the time, but creating that motto as I climbed those stairs would become a defining moment in my career. Those sixteen words would light my way for years to come.

Through these words I can articulate my goals about being student centered. I intend to listen to students and not talk at them. I intend to use a participatory approach to leadership rather than a top-down one. I am a person who will reverse a bad decision because I can see my occasional fallibility.

Through those words I can explain my strengths in the area of personal compassion and my desire never to be judgmental. I know that I am able to recognize that my teachers are parents, spouses, and children first and employees second. I know that I am able to walk in the shoes of that angry parent who challenges me out of love for his child. I know that I am able to empathize with the reluctant student who has to endure hardships in life that I can barely imagine. In addition, through the notion of understanding, rather than guessing, I can expound on my vast experiences in educational leadership. Before making decisions—tough or easy ones—I survey for answers, ask trusted colleagues for advice, and, most importantly, seek facts.

The interview started as most do. I was a bit nervous, as was the interviewing committee. The questions they were asking had not yet led us to a comfortable flow of conversation. I think that the fourth question asked had to do with my philosophy of leadership. Without hesitation I replied, "I strive to listen more than I talk, care more than I judge, and understand more than I guess."

I didn't think I needed to say anything beyond that to convince the interviewing committee that I stood for something important. Of course, I expanded on the answer, but I believed that the foundation of my work could be seen through that motto. I didn't get the job. It was not meant to be. But that motto has stuck with me ever since. I have used it over and over again to explain who I am and the way that I see leadership.

It has become part of my everyday work, because in reality it is part of my personal makeup. I believe this simple motto, scratched on a yellow legal pad in the front seat of my car some fifteen years ago, is who I have become. It is personally and professionally empowering to know what you really stand for!

Teacher Leaders

Leadership Has Little to Do with One's Title

Webster's New World Dictionary defines a leader as one who shows the way or guides. Although the same words are not used in the definition of a teacher, it is not much of a stretch to see the similarities. Teachers have to be leaders if they are to impart knowledge. They are out front directing their students.

In devoting the second section of this book to leadership, I want to be very clear that I am not limiting myself to accounts of school administrators. Leadership is not really a function of a person's title; leadership is about showing the way and guiding. Teachers as well as parents, coaches, even students can be leaders. Leaders need to know what is, what should be, and what can be. These skills are just as essential for teachers as they are for the mayor of New York City. This story focuses on teacher leadership both inside and outside the classroom.

Warren Bennis suggests that leaders must empower others, give direction, be trustworthy, and provide hope. These ideas form the foundation of any conversation about leadership. As teachers work to create dynamic classrooms, they must have credibility, the ability to convince others, great communication skills, and compassion. I believe teachers can be leaders outside of their classrooms as well.

Just as it is logical to assume that high levels of student engagement will lead to greater student achievement, the same holds true for teachers. The more teachers feel empowered, the more likely they are to feel ownership for the school. I believe the participatory leadership leads to quality schools. The involvement of many broadens the base of leadership and helps to create shared community beliefs. It develops teachers who perceive themselves as leaders. The more principals can involve teachers in the leadership of the schools, the more teachers will be inspired to leave the seclusion of their classrooms and contribute to the school as a whole. Most of the reform efforts I have been involved in as a principal depended heavily on teacher leadership. The faculties in each school where I have worked have had ample staff capable of quality leadership. All that they needed was permission, direction, and inspiration.

Teachers have to be nurtured and inspired to lead. I have supported the idea of term limits for department chairpersons, which in turn can widen the leadership base of a school. This idea is driven by the need to have more teachers experience administrative roles as well as the need to revitalize some stagnated departments. In most schools there are no term limits for department leaders, which prohibits other teachers from experiencing and benefiting from leadership opportunities.

I have also come to believe in the value of employing quasi-administrators as a means to create strong leadership in schools. Quasi-administrators are half-time teachers and half-time administrators. I currently have three such people on my staff. There are a number of benefits to this idea. First, it provides faculty members with real administrative authority. This reduces the likelihood that teachers and administrators will assume adversarial roles. Second, a quasi position allows individuals to experience administrative responsibilities without having to relinquish their teaching positions. This allows some of the best teachers to test the administrative waters, which opens up the possibility that some of them may decide to pursue full-time positions in administration. Most important, the school and leadership team becomes the beneficiary of their great skills and passionate work.

I have spoken with many teachers across the country about inspirational leadership. It is truly a rewarding experience when someone who hears me speak decides that administration might be worth a look because I somehow changed their perception of what the work of a school administrator entails. The young educators I have met in my travels and those with whom I have had the privilege of working seem to relish the idea of making a difference. They make me hopeful that there is a new and better generation of school leaders emerging, leaders who can inspire and provide hope.

Much has been written about the potential shortage of school administrators as current school leaders approach retirement age. Working to create teacher leaders today will go a long way in minimizing this issue.

A Weird Idea That Worked

One Size Does Not Fit All

No matter how long I stay in education, I am continually amazed by how little we learn from our mistakes. We have all heard the advice that we have to find something to love in every child. But that advice is often hard to follow in the workings of today's schools.

My first principalship presented me with many challenges. One student in particular tested everyone's patience. For the sake of privacy, I will refer to him as Joey, although that really wasn't his name. Joey was a fourth grade terror. He did not work, he did not listen, and he did not appear to care. By mid October there was not a teacher in the building—including the principal—who could get Joey to respond. We had tried everything. My lectures to Joey about appropriate behavior fell on deaf ears. He would physically plug both his ears with his fingers and make a humming sound as I tried to preach goodness into his head. The psychological testing that we scheduled shed little light on this youngster. In fact, during the testing Joey conveniently found the light switch, darkened the room, and blocked the proctor's path to the switch! The test administrator reported that he could not complete the evaluation.

Everyone had the same take on Joey: he was incorrigible. All of the adults in the building spent their energy catching Joey doing wrong. They would run down to the office to report his latest incident and share their growing frustration that this young man was out of control. I, in turn, would meet with Joey or his parents, issue a consequence, and know that the cycle would continue the next day.

Eventually, after all of my ideas and options had been used up, I came up with a weird idea. I delivered a memo to staff indicating that unless Joey was hurting himself or someone else, his behavior was to be totally ignored. The teachers' room erupted with criticism:

"How could you ask me to act as if this boy were invisible?"

"Have you lost your mind?"

"What kind of disciplinarian is this new principal going to be?"

"How could you give a fourth grader the run of the school?"

Despite the negative reactions, the teachers did follow my directive. If Joey was hanging out in the hall or staring out the window, then everyone just ignored him. He was not escorted down to my office every fifteen minutes for doing something outrageous. In fact, he did not get referred to me at all for the next several days. The plan might have drawn a lot of criticism, but at least I got a few days off from wrath of Joey. At least I was enjoying myself.

Three days into the plan, Joey's classroom teacher called me to her room. Her class was just a short walk from my office. In anticipation of more bad news, I developed a plan as I walked down the corridor. This was Joey's class. He had to be out of control again. I had to figure out how I could remove him from the class. I decided that I would enter the classroom and ask the teacher and all of the other students to move to the library. With this plan, Joey wouldn't have an audience to perform for. I might be able to get him to listen to me. I turned into Joey's room with that plan, but not wholly convinced that it would work.

I was surprised when the teacher greeted me at the door with a smile. She whispered that she thought I might want to see this. Joey was sitting at his desk doing his work! She indicated that she had let him wander around the room for the past three days and worked hard not to respond to any of his behaviors. From what she could conclude, he had tired of not getting any attention. Joey had come in that morning and just started being a student. She praised his first piece of work; he smiled and started another assignment.

The cycle of Joey's getting all the attention for being disruptive was replaced with his being recognized for doing things right. He thrived on the positive attention and went on to make the honor roll that quarter. Although he still had an occasional outburst, the weird idea to make the incorrigible Joey invisible had worked.

In education we have to recognize that one size does not fit all. In my efforts to work toward creating a school for each child,

I have tried many weird ideas to change patterns of failure into patterns of success. Joey was on a path of no return. We had the courage to try something different. Many students need multiple invitations to embark on the road to success. The responsibility of extending those invitations goes hand in hand with being an educator.

Inspirational Models

Leading Through Common Sense, Loyalty, and Persistence

It would be a bit of a stretch to include my parents as models of leadership—unless you really knew them. From afar, people would look at my father, Roger, and dismiss his contribution to a leadership formula based on his third grade education. My mother, Laurette, would gain even less attention, given that she did not work outside the home. Their contribution to my leadership style, however, deserves top billing. As my first teachers, they made a huge contribution to how I see the world and my work within it.

Roger was simply my hero. Despite his lack of formal schooling, he built a successful life and business around some very basic values that would hold up well today. Common sense, allegiance, and persistence would be found between the lines of any statement about leadership for success. These are the things that I remember most about my father.

As a French Canadian immigrant, he came to the United States two years prior to my birth. He started out working in the woods with his brother, operating a two-man chain saw—a life that had little to offer. One hot humid day while on a break from their logging, they looked at each other and realized that something better had to be out there. They made a pact to find an English-speaking interpreter (who turned out to be their mailman) who could accompany them to a bank and help them borrow the money to start up a construction business. Twenty-five years later, at age fifty-two, my father retired. He had developed a very successful home-building company and had built more than three hundred fifty homes. He went on to live twenty comfortable years in retirement before losing a two-year battle to cancer at the age of seventy-three.

I remember many things about my father's business, but several things stand out above the rest. The first has to do with loyalty. He never had a crew of more than seven workers, and there was a sense of family within the organization. Whenever he sold a house, his workers would get a bonus. In some cases it was money or tools, but it also could have been dental work for one of the employee's children. I remember hanging around the job site as a kid noticing how the workers stayed on task even when my dad was off doing errands. As with every occupation a bit of coasting might occur, but these men knew about allegiance to my father. There was no union, nor was one necessary. My dad took care of his crew, and they did their work with pride.

I also recall the business instincts my father exhibited. Without much formal education, he relied on common sense to guide his decisions. He had a way of taking complex questions or problems and factoring them down into pretty simple yes or no determinations. These determinations had more to do with humanity than with the carrying load of a box beam. He somehow knew about economies and efficiencies in the construction trade, and he built homes that people wanted and could afford. I often marvel at how most decisions that I make in educational settings really are grounded in common sense—common sense that my father modeled for me, time and time again.

Another vivid memory I have of my father's work was his persistence in the face of challenges. I remember events such as the time a concrete foundation caved in, a vital piece of machinery broke down, or an unanticipated storm came in. Each of these obstacles was met with a stiffening of the upper lip and a determination to overcome them.

If my father were alive today, he would look at most of the stories in this book as fairly unremarkable. The comfort zone for an educational leader might pale in comparison to that of non-English speaking immigrant starting a business. Dad would look at the clash between inspiration and legislation that occurs among my crew (faculty and staff members) with disbelief. He would ask the question that we should all ask: "Where is the importance of keeping loyalty and humanity at the center of our schools?" The same disbelief would surface as he discovered the mandates and red tape that encircle my work. He would ask: "Isn't this supposed to be about the kids?" Following those critical impressions, he would express pleasure regarding the level of common sense and the intensity of purpose that I apply to my work. He would see some of himself in me.

My mother's story extends the notion that persistence is a valuable leadership trait. For the majority of her life she has been wholeheartedly a stay-at-home, Franco-American housewife. Her role was to raise five children, create a happy home, and support her husband's business (she was my father's bookkeeper). She filled each role in expert fashion. Her five children all became productive adults. She can boast of having ten grandchildren and eight great-grandchildren. Her life today, at age eighty-five, still very much revolves around a loving family.

What applies to this book about my mother occurred long before I was born. In 1936, my mother was a school teacher in Quebec, Canada. At age seventeen she taught in a one-room schoolhouse. Her school had fifty-three students ranging in age from five to fourteen. As unbelievable as it sounds by today's standards, she was the lone worker (you could stretch it to say the lone adult) at this school. There was no principal, no educational technician, no school psychologist, no custodian, no special educator, no security officer, no counselor, no social worker—just my mother. It is truly entertaining to discuss with her the problems that I encounter in my work. Here are a few examples:

- Her understanding of cooperative learning is that it is a means of survival. For example, at her school the big kids helped the little ones. She was shocked to learn that today this practice is often questioned by parents or occurs so rarely that it is considered an innovation.

- When asked about discipline, my mother notes that the few children who did act out had to split the firewood, stoke the stove, and clean the school. She is quick to point out that there were no real problems. She has certainly never heard of attention deficit disorder.

- Standardized testing happened back then too. My mother mentioned that one boy, who had difficulty learning, stayed at home when the testing officials came to assess her school. This certainly would not occur with today's

No Child Left Behind legislation. By the same token, my mother's school did not include children with disabilities. In any event, her annual yearly progress was measured by the academic and social growth of her students.

♦ Any discussion about technology in schools brings a blank stare from my mother. She considers all of this "computer stuff" to be an unexplainable miracle.

♦ When asked why she had so many students in her school, she indicates that she had accepted two fourteen-year-old children whom she wasn't supposed to take. They needed an extra year of learning. The rest were simply the school-aged children in that district.

Mom taught at this school for five years before being married and moving out of the area. We marvel at how different the world is sixty-four years later. Perhaps then, being a seventeen-year-old in charge of an entire school with more than fifty students was not uncommon. By current standards, it would be totally outside of anyone's comfort zone. My mother will tell you that having five children in a seven-and-one-half-year span was even more difficult. Her teaching experience was her training ground for motherhood. From my vantage point, the training was a success.

I have learned much from my parents, and those lessons have found their way into the core principles of my leadership. These include the application of common sense, the importance of loyalty, and the need for persistence. And, above all, I live with the reality that both my parents took remarkable risks, which appear to tower over those mentioned in this book. They left their comfort zone and persevered.

Success Is in the Details
Taking the Time Pays Huge Dividends

Shortly after I arrived at Kennebunk High School, I engaged in a conversation with parents about graduation procedures. This conversation occurred during a parent/principal forum that is held every month. I asked about commencement to get the parents' opinions about how well we honored our graduates. Their responses led me to conclude that a lot of work had to be done to elevate our graduation traditions. The following story conveys what I learned about what graduation was like for the parents and the community and how we worked to improve the situation.

I was surprised when the father of a recent graduate told of having to arrive at graduation two hours early in order to find a good seat. All I could picture was nice people arguing and fighting over who would sit where. He spoke of the gymnasium being packed one and one-half hours prior to the ceremony and how the temperature in the room rose five to ten degrees every twenty minutes. By the time the graduates started marching, the temperature in the room was in the high nineties. Other parents started contributing to this image that he had depicted for me.

One parent talked about knowing of a graduate's mother who could not get into the gym because it was filled to capacity one hour before the ceremony was scheduled to start. Can you imagine having to stand outside as your child receives a high school diploma?

Another parent related how hard it was for her elderly mother to sit through a three-hour ceremony when her daughter graduated several years earlier. It was becoming obvious to me that high school graduation at Kennebunk High School was not a family friendly affair. And these observations were just the start of the parents' concerns.

Parents were frustrated that the scheduled time for graduation prohibited their having family outings. People who traveled from great distances to attend had little time to spend with the families or the graduates. They had to be at the school by 11:00 AM just to get in, and the ceremony usually ended after 4:00 PM. After spending nearly five hours in a sweltering facility, families would try to squeeze in an abbreviated graduation party after that, because the graduates had to be back at school by 5:30 PM to leave for Project Graduation, a chemical-free, all-night senior party.

The parents also talked about some graduation procedures that caused hard feelings in the community. For example, because of handicap accessibility issues, at least for one year, the graduates were seated at floor level, and most people in the audience could not see the graduates. No wonder there was a mad scramble for the best seats.

Another parent complained that the presentation of scholarships went on forever, further highlighting that this portion of the program was almost more about the presenters of each scholarship than it was about the students who received them. Last, parents mentioned the horrendous traffic issues after graduation with everyone trying to get off-site and back home so that they could be with their families.

As I left the meeting that night I was certain of two things. First, I knew that something had to be done to change graduation procedures for the sake of the community. Second, I knew that whatever changes I proposed, I needed to be able to count on strong backing from this group of frustrated school supporters. The changes that had to be made would uproot some long-sanding traditions and upset a number of people. I would need these parents in my corner.

The following month I went to the parent/principal forum with an eight-step plan aimed at addressing the concerns that parents had raised. The following summary highlights the key points.

1. We would change the time of graduation to 3:00 PM, which would allow families to have morning and lunch time for their gatherings.

2. We would have randomly assigned ticketed seating. This arrangement which would eliminate the war over seating

and allow us to open the doors at 2:00 PM, which would help us maintain a cooler facility.

3. The graduates would be on a raised platform so that they could be seen regardless of where in the gymnasium people were sitting.

4. The length of the graduation ceremony would be reduced to 90 minutes or less.

5. Scholarships and presentations of awards would be moved to Class Night, and these events would be streamlined through the elimination of all outside presenters.

6. The entire commencement ceremony would feature only senior speakers and the graduates receiving diplomas. We would attempt to honor all graduates equally.

7. Graduates would not be allowed to go home between the end of graduation and their departure for Project Graduation. If this was to be a chemical-free event, then the past practice of letting students leave made no sense.

8. Following the ceremony there would be a reception on site, organized by the parents of the junior class, to encourage families to gather at school rather than dashing away. This event would allow the community to share in the celebration and start a new tradition of involving the parents of junior students in the graduation process.

When I presented this plan to my parent group, there was no skepticism. They recognized that the changes outlined addressed the concerns they had raised a month earlier. I asked them to provide me with visible and moral support as I pursued making these changes, and they agreed.

As difficult as this eight-point plan seemed at the outset, the changes all happened without too much contention. Perhaps the timing was perfect, because one would think that changing traditions would uncover a great deal of resistance. The superintendent of schools, the school committee, the faculty, the students, and the community all trusted that these changes would lead to improvement. The fact that we had made so many other successful changes during my first year at this school probably helped with that trust. We had developed credibility through a long list of positive reforms.

The outcome of this plan was awesome. Each of the pieces worked well, and commencement week was a huge success. The process did not occur without some challenges, however.

I remember a difficult phone conversation with a government official who was upset that he would not be able to present an award at graduation. As hard as it was, I did not cave in. Commencement was about the graduates, not political exposure. The same concern surfaced among members of the Alumni Association. Although they understood the need for the adjustments, they grieved the loss of being able to present. We simply had to find other ways to give this important organization the recognition it deserved.

There was also the question of placing the graduates on a raised platform. We found we could not afford to rent such a huge structure on an annual basis, so we built it instead. Luckily I was able to convince my superiors that this had to be done. We found a staff member with carpentry skills and a huge commitment to the school to spearhead the project. The expenses incurred were only slightly greater than the cost of rental, yet the school gained a permanent structure.

Perhaps the most difficult issue was the assigned seating. The people who helped me with this enormous task questioned the wisdom of spending five or six hours during such a busy time on this detail. We literally had a chart of the eight hundred floor seats and assigned a name to each one. We also accommodated split families, handicapped seating, and other special circumstances. This task was not easy.

A number of parents called to say they would need thirty tickets, yet we were allowing each graduate only ten or twelve tickets. We calmly explained why we needed to limit the number of tickets issued. We assured them, however, that their child could end up with as many as sixteen or eighteen tickets. We also encouraged them to invite some of their friends and relatives to attend Class Night instead of graduation, reminding them that the ceremonies would be quite similar. Despite these contentious conversations, in the end everyone appeared satisfied. Not one parent complained that he or she could not get in or had not received enough tickets.

One of the school's former principals approached me shortly after graduation and congratulated me for having succeeded at making the changes he had always wanted to make during his tenure. He indicated that he simply could not get the support needed to make these changes happen. Although I could understand his dilemma, I couldn't help but think that the success I had was in the details. We had gathered compelling data that highlighted a need for change. We then formulated a comprehensive plan that addressed all the concerns. And, most important, we had the conviction to attend to the tedious details that would make the plan work. I never second guessed the time I spent assigning seats, having the raisers built, or meeting with junior parents. Success is often in the details.

Timing Is Almost Everything

"You Got to Know When to Hold Them, Know When to Fold Them, Know When to Walk Away, Know When to Run"*

At a conference many years ago I heard a speaker indicate that "The Gambler," sung by Kenny Rogers, should be the theme song of all principals. Certainly, accurately reading the cards you are dealt and instinctively knowing how to proceed are a big part of leadership. The following story shows the fine line between winning and losing. It is a story of a hand well played.

I have never been a big fan of parent–teacher conferences. It seems that the only parents we ever see at such events are the parents of our top students. Parents of struggling or reluctant learners rarely show up. In all of the schools where I have worked, only about seventeen percent to fifty percent of parents attended conferences—not exactly impressive statistics. What bothers me most, however, is the fact that students are not involved in the process. Parents come to school while their child stays home and watches television. Teachers meet with parents and give them insight into their child's learning, yet the student often never hears the information.

From a teacher's perspective, conferences go one of two ways. Either one is swamped with fifty or sixty ten-minute meetings or one has little or no business. The teachers of the most academic students feel that these brief meetings do little to validate their work or the work of their students. The stress of holding meeting after meeting with little chance of meaningful dialogue leaves teachers longing for a better process. Conversely, the teachers who really want to see certain parents because of the support they could provide usually have a poor response. It is obvious that parents who need improved home–school communication the most are the ones who are least likely to attend.

During the process of writing a Comprehensive School Reform grant at Leavitt Area High School, a team of three grant

---

*Lyrics by Don Schiltz (1976).

writers, which included two wonderful teachers and me, addressed the problem of ineffective parent conferences. Just as we were ready to present the faculty with our final grant proposal, one of the grant writers came in with an idea to have student-led conferences. We had worked for the better part of a month on this grant proposal, and it had not been easy. One of our teachers was a pioneer—someone who heard an idea and just couldn't wait to try it. The other teacher was more black and white, the type who needed to be sure of the direction we were heading in. I was somewhere in the middle and faced the challenge of balancing the different styles of these two great teachers while at the same time being concerned about gaining faculty support.

When the idea of student-led conferences entered the picture late in the process, it created some contention. The pioneer who had thought of this approach wanted to add it to our proposal. She felt that it blended with our other ideas and simply had to be done. The other teacher believed that including it would be a big mistake because it would diminish faculty support for our proposal. I was in my familiar place—one of considerable discomfort—right in the middle between two strong-willed teachers. We brought the idea to the faculty, and it turned out that they were not going to support this idea. Therefore, we excluded it from our grant application. The more cautious teacher had been right about the lack of support, at least for the time being.

The next year, as we reworked our grant proposal, the notion of student-led conferences had started to gain considerable support. Once faculty members had taken some time to consider the idea, they started warming up to the possibilities. We discovered that the concept of student-led conferences was very much in concert with other grant initiatives. In fact, we came to the conclusion that this format for conferences would bolster most areas of our reform efforts. The pioneer had been right all along—we just had not been ready to recognize it.

We had members of our leadership team attend a planning seminar that summer. Going into this seminar, we knew that student-led conferences were going to happen. We just didn't know how. I remember giving a small subcommittee some non-negotiables about these conferences (essentially that student-led conferences were going to happen) and sending them off to plan. They came back with a conceptual plan of how this was going to happen and the idea that we should get a group of teachers together for a few days in August to finalize the plan.

Although student-led conferences were already used in other areas of the country, we decided to build this program to fit our needs. We consciously made a decision not to borrow ideas on how to do this from other schools. A committee of five or six teachers developed a graphic organizer for student-led conferences that summer. It was based on the concept that students would be the central focus of parent conferences and that they would be in control of the meetings with their parents. Their advisor teacher would be there to support their efforts. We wanted them to reflect on where they were educationally, where they wanted to be, and what they needed to do to get there. This approach was going to be a significant departure from our traditional parent–teacher conferences.

The school community made a tremendous commitment to the new program. We had the drama students develop a video on what a good student-led conference would look like, which was viewed by the entire school during advisory period. We spent several hours in advisories having students prepare for and practice their presentations. I sent three different mailings home to parents explaining the new format and emphasizing the need for one hundred percent participation by parents. We continually fielded questions from parents and teachers who wanted to go back to the old way before the new process had even begun. There was skepticism that parents would not have their needs met unless they could meet directly with their students' teachers.

In response to this concern we had an open house early in the year so that parents could actually follow their child's schedule for an evening. This, we believed, would allow parents to put a name with a face, understand course expectations, and open lines of communication between home and school. Nearly twenty-five percent of the parents attended, which was a pleasant surprise.

As the date of student-led conferences approached, panic began setting in. Students were under stress about the work, teachers were fearful that parents would not come, and parents were apprehensive. The panic was unnecessary.

We had more than a ninety percent turnout—a staggering increase over the mere seventeen percent attendance a year earlier. Given the fact that many of these parents had never stepped foot into Leavitt High School, this was a huge change for the better.

Our students rose to the occasion and presented a well-organized, thoughtful presentation of their work at school. We realized that the objective of putting them in the center of the process had been met.

The parents were extremely appreciative of the new format. Many marveled at the responsibility their child was taking for his or her learning. Some parents even expressed delight that they finally heard their child espouse (and own) goals and strategies that they had been preaching for years.

The advisory teachers were relieved that their fear of being put on the spot by parents who wanted to know more about a particular course did not materialize. In fact, only a handful of parents left the student-led conference requesting a follow-up meeting with a particular teacher, which was an option that had been made available to them given the initial concerns about the new format.

We surveyed nearly seven hundred parents, sixty teachers, and seven hundred students at the end of conferences and found that ninety-eight percent of teachers and parents and seventy percent of the students were impressed with the process. This was a clear indication that the students did most of the work.

An idea that had failed to gain faculty support a year earlier had become, arguably, the greatest success we had ever accomplished. Just the fact that we got such a high percentage of parents to attend was impressive. That they strongly supported the process was a bonus.

In the next school year Leavitt faculty members refined the program and again had great success. By then I had moved on to Kennebunk High School, and in my second year there we instituted student-led conferences. We took the Leavitt plan and tweaked it to fit the new school's needs. The program was again a huge success.

The graphic organizers continue to be improved annually and are being utilized in a number of schools around the state. We have even extended our influence to a wider audience. While at a conference in Providence, Rhode Island, I attended a session on student-led conferences. To my amazement, one of the participants pulled out a copy of the Kennebunk student-led conference organizer. We continually receive calls requesting copies of our work. We have made an admirable impact with this idea that almost didn't happen.

Educational leadership sometimes involves more than good ideas. Timing is also important. Had we forced the issue of student-led conferences when our faculty wasn't ready, it might have failed. Yet, had we abandoned the idea based on early reluctance, our communities never would have experienced this wonderful innovation.

A Tipping Point

Develop an Ability to Synthesize Information

The origins of my journey as an educational leader can probably be traced back to a moment some thirty years ago. Out of context, the incident would appear trivial, but its events led to this defining moment—what I call the tipping point in my development.

After teaching and coaching for two years in a small community in rural Maine, I decided to apply for a job in a larger school. My career goals focused on coaching basketball. A move to the Class A rank, following some success in the Class C rank, seemed logical. The high school I applied to was brand new and was to serve students from communities that had in the past sent their students to other districts. The principal had been on the payroll for a full year prior to the opening of the facility. He had the luxury of building a faculty and developing programs from scratch.

My application for a physical education/coaching position led to an interview that I thought was less than stellar. I knew little about the proposed school. The principal seemed to have little interest in my coaching skills. Most of his interview questions focused on my educational philosophy and programming, which I felt ill-equipped to answer. The responses I gave to the few questions that I could answer seemed to raise differing points of view from the interviewer. As I drove back home, I was certain that I was not going to be offered the job. To my surprise, by the time I reached home the principal had called to welcome me to his faculty.

Although I taught for six years in that school, which was on the cutting edge of educational reform, the beginning period was stressful. The hand-selected faculty comprised seventy top-notch educators. I saw myself as number seventy-one. To me, all of my colleagues seemed to have doctoral degrees from Harvard or some other major university. My degree came from a tiny state school. I was a physical education teacher with little background or interest in core academics. My high school and college transcripts were an embarrassment. I was only in my early twenties with few worldly experiences, so picturing myself as an equal to other members of this elite faculty was difficult. I was also extremely self-conscious about speaking in public. I had shades of a French accent that embarrassed me. And my basketball team's thirty-eight game losing streak did little to help my self-esteem. My perceived value to this high-powered diverse faculty was simply nonexistent.

Almost equally void was my understanding of the educational reforms we were trying to accomplish. The time was the mid 1970s, and the school was experimenting with all sorts of new educational innovations. Our school had an open concept design. We were implementing a humanistic approach to education with an advisory program at its core. The diversity and background of the faculty made it difficult to achieve consensus on educational questions. Our faculty meetings and staff development activities were battle grounds where strong personalities and philosophies clashed.

All faculty members had to spend the week before the school's grand opening in teacher workshops. The district had hired consultants to help us bond as a new faculty.

I can still remember the first activity they had us participate in. It was called the "name game." We had to state our name and everyone else's names from memory. I still break out in a sweat when I think back on this workshop. I was so overwhelmed by the group that I could barely remember my own name. My discomfort was magnified by the fact that I was on crutches at the time. I had suffered a broken bone in my foot while folding up the school's trampoline. I spent the first day in predictable conversations.

"Hi! My name is Nelson. I teach P.E."

"What happened to your foot?"

"Oh, nothing serious. I broke it on the trampoline."

I would leave each of these conversations even more convinced that I belonged at the bottom of this ecosystem.

The next game we played was called the "airplane game," which was followed by the "shoe relay." With each activity I grew more self-conscious. And with each activity I observed faculty who were supposed to be bonding growing even more polarized. The principal, who had selected his staff, seemed to have purposefully hired people with a wide array of views. Some were clearly not excited about the process approach to staff development. Others were thrilled over it. I was simply petrified.

The idea of reaching decisions about our new school through faculty consensus caused even more contention. We had about seventy-five educators arranged in a huge circle debating issues to death. A few confident faculty members dominated the discussions. I sat in silent anguish, not daring to speak. My frustration mounted with every meeting. With each discussion came the battle between adopting a new idea versus retreating toward time-tested beliefs.

I cannot remember any point in my career where faculty members worked so hard and so long. Yet we appeared to accomplish very little. The weekly staff meetings lasted well into the supper hour. Our energy was being sapped—not so much by the time commitment but by the stress of demoralizing debates.

In the middle of the second year of the school's existence, faculty members found themselves in a heated debate over our struggling advisory program. We had invested a great deal of time and resources to this program, but it was not accomplishing what we had hoped. One-third of the staff had established wonderful relationships with their advisees. They were well suited to student-centered programming, and the notion of serving as advisors came naturally to them. An equal number of staff felt ill suited for advisory and, perhaps, subconsciously refused to invest themselves in the program. I, along with the remainder of the teachers, stood somewhere in the middle. I had established a great rapport with my students, yet I wasn't sure that I was really implementing the program as I should.

The faculty discussions about the advisory program followed predictable philosophical lines. Those who were comfortable with the program wanted no change. They simply felt that the rest of the faculty needed to commit to doing what they were doing. The opposite camp wanted the entire program thrown out, or at least turned upside down and restarted. The faculty stuck in the middle watched in silent frustration as the debate raged on.

During the third meeting dominated by this subject of advisory I became fed up. We had spent hours debating this subject, yet we were nowhere near reaching a consensus. In fact, the three or four hours of discussion had not yielded one proposal worthy of consideration.

Suddenly I meekly raised my hand, indicating that I had something to say. When I finally got the floor I was a wreck! The emotions I was experiencing made my voice crack. I was so nervous about addressing this group of people, for whom I still felt considerable awe, that I began to stutter. The sheer realization that all eyes were on me brought on feelings of desperation. Why in the world had I raised my hand? I had already forgotten what I wanted to say. As I stumbled on, my comment was something like this, although I am sure that it was not nearly this articulate:

> I have been listening to everyone for a long time, and I think I have an idea that might provide some type of compromise. Some of you like how your advisories are running. Why don't we let you continue them? Some of you want to start over. Why don't we set up a system in which you can? All of us want the advisory program to get better. Why don't we use a reshuffling draft, based on student wishes, as an event aimed at recommitting everyone to this program?

After I finished my remarks the room fell silent. I was in a panic. Why had I been so stupid? I should have known better—these people would not even give my idea the time of day.

One of the faculty leaders who frequently spoke at meetings broke the silence by stating in a surprised, but appreciative, way, "I think Nelson might have just outlined a plan that will work." To my surprise, another outspoken teacher, one who was on the opposite side of the advisory issue, said, "This idea seems to value everyone's point of view. Let's form a committee to draw up a proposal."

Minutes later a committee was being appointed to finalize this plan. Of course, I was selected as the chairperson. This was an appointment I wanted nothing to do with, but the shame of saying no was too great. In an instant, I had gone from a silent, frustrated, tag-along in the faculty process to the chairperson of an important steering committee. Our committee came back to the faculty, and our plan received final approval and was put into place.

Several months later the faculty were working on improving our meeting protocols. They decided to establish a position of faculty moderator to direct the flow of the meetings. I was nominated to this post. The person who spoke on my behalf noted my strengths in assimilating information and finding compromises in tough situations. To my surprise, I was elected to the post.

At the time, I thought that maybe people voted for me because they thought I would be harmless. Today, I realize that by taking the chance to reach beyond my comfort zone, my skills in synthesizing information and finding solutions were beginning to be recognized. The moment of frustration that compelled me to speak up was the beginning of my work in educational leadership—a real tipping point in my journey into administration. My emerging skill of assimilating information would soon help to define the educator I would become.

Sometimes Wrong Is Right

Find Ways to Honor Your Superstars and Raise the Bar for Everyone

I have learned over the years that teachers hate to hear lectures from their leaders about people who are doing things poorly if they are doing things correctly. It is demoralizing for a teacher who constantly turns his or her grades in before the deadline to hear an administrator chewing out the entire faculty because other teachers were late. These exemplary teachers want administrators to speak directly to the people who have dropped the ball. To subject the people who are doing their job correctly to reprimands is fundamentally wrong.

The converse is true. I have found that by praising people who do what is expected, one can raise the standards for those who are not working up to snuff. Someone once coined this concept "the notion of honoring superstars." I have used this idea often in my work, and members of my leadership team constantly remind one another about this important approach. We are careful not to send out memos or general reprimands. However, there are exceptions to every rule. This story illustrates a time when I broke this rule and reprimanded the entire faculty. It was a huge risk and took a fair amount of courage, but the outcome proved that sometimes the opposite of a rule might work.

We were experiencing some problems at faculty meetings with respectful and professional behavior. I addressed the issue one person at a time to avoid the trap of lecturing to my superstars. During one particular meeting a few incidents occurred that showed me that our disintegrating faculty meetings were starting to affect everyone. Usually, our meetings were pretty good, but over time we had become complacent. In the days and weeks that followed the meeting, several staff members approached me about how embarrassed they were becoming at faculty meetings. It was clear to me that they probably didn't know that I was addressing the problem with specific offenders. It also became evident that my method of addressing these minor problems did not appear to be working. By not addressing the offensive behavior in a public way, I was frustrating my superstars.

I met with my leadership team about this situation. I also asked several faculty members for advice. Everyone agreed that something had to be done, but every possible solution had potentially negative ramifications. One morning I got up early and headed into school with the intent of writing a position paper on faculty meetings. The following is the content of the paper that I wrote.

* * *

To: All Staff
From: Nelson Beaudoin
Re: Faculty Meeting Reflections

Are our faculty meetings demoralizing or uplifting? Do they feel more like a battleground or peace talks? Do you see them as an intrusion or a time of productivity?

I am compelled to write this paper as a result of a significant number of our staff approaching me in recent weeks to express concern about our faculty meetings. I do not intend for this to be a tongue lashing towards anyone, but rather a validation of majority sentiment. We need to move from good to GREAT!

As you read this, it is important that you recognize that this is not about me. Although many of the conversations about faculty meetings were prompted by individual staff concerns about how I was holding up, I am pleased to announce I am doing just fine. I do not drive home after meetings wishing I were working somewhere else. Most of the time I leave feeling that I handled things pretty well. Although this is a biased view, I think I am pretty good on my feet and generally treat all of you graciously and with respect.

As I reflect on faculty meetings, I do sometimes wonder what they would look like to an outside observer. If the observer looked at one of our meetings in the context of a classroom, what would be seen? What are we modeling?

It would not go unnoticed that a handful of eager people arrive early. These early birds are followed by the masses that cross the threshold as the bell is ringing. Finally, six or seven people filter in late—some with an apologetic demeanor and others seemingly without a care.

The observer would see a majority of people sitting in chairs. He or she would, I am sure, notice eight or ten people sitting or lounging in the far reaches of the room. As the meeting progressed, the observer might make a number of discoveries such as the following:

- A noticeable number of side conversations take place.
- Some conversations appear to be mockeries of the proceedings or particular speakers.
- Among the vast audience, only a small percentage speak while some speak several times.
- Some speakers generate a group response: giggling, rolling eyes, or dismissive inattention.
- Some of the people sit quietly, looking occasionally at the clock, waiting for their sentence to be served.
- Most listen intently, fighting through the distractions, taking the "company" line and trying to be engaged.
- Occasionally, there might be a group laugh, or a consensus attitude might ripple through the room.
- More frequently, participants squirm with personal discomfort about the direction of the conversation.

If this represents what others might see, then it would appear that we are not really modeling what we expect to happen in our classrooms.

One staff member asked me the other day if it was just the Kennebunk High School faculty that had meetings like this. I felt qualified to answer, based on the fact that this is the eighth school I've worked at. My answer was no! You can change the names, faces, and chairs, but what you see here is pretty much what you see everywhere. Yet this response begs the question—couldn't we be different or better than the rest? Nevertheless, I tried to justify what's happening to this staff member by saying that people are busy, stressed, selfish by nature, overworked, etc.

In thinking about my answer, I find that my thoughts jump to my early days at K.H.S. The focus then was on the information I was receiving about faculty meetings prior to my arrival. If the information I received was correct, faculty meetings were not peaceful, uplifting, or productive. Many of you e-mailed me or spoke to me about how refreshing our meetings had become under my leadership. I still occasionally receive those comments, although I admittedly have run out of gas in terms of planning faculty skits or games. I have also gone away from recognition, as this seemed to create jealously or strife.

Have we forgotten the not so distant past and come to measure today's events with no memory of days gone by? Or are we just coming full circle and repeating history?

A number of questions arise as I think about what we can do to become a great faculty in terms of meetings and working together. The answers, however, are not jumping out of my head. I do know that we can make great progress by simply looking in the mirror. If we see some ugliness, can we commit to fixing it? I doubt if some of the things I mentioned earlier are pathological. They are simply habits that can be changed. I am sure that some of the things I've said will make you uncomfortable, but I am also sure that this means I am doing my job. Do we want to be good, or do we want to be great?

I next would like to go on another little journey with you, again related to faculty meetings. If you were to ask me what I was trying to do here, I would answer quickly and confidently, using the terms *participatory leadership, faculty and student voice, and empowerment of teachers*. How many of you would agree with that notion?

In a way, it is a target that does not fit well into most of your comfort zones. Many of you see me as the boss. You would like for me to tell you what to do. Others of you value the idea of empowerment, but when push comes to shove, you've got too much on your plate to really embrace it. Still others have no use for anything administrative and, consequently, wouldn't recognize it even if you had all the say in the world.

At the last meeting, our target was to get faculty consensus for a plan for late-start Wednesdays. We had come up with a framework to work from, and we voted on two proposed revisions. It is interesting to note that I proposed both of these revisions. Although my intent was to have you develop the plan, to perhaps create ownership, you basically decided to accept three of my ideas. For most of you, this was probably okay because you trusted that my ideas were grounded in faculty ideas and data. For a small minority, however, this decision will become a future excuse . . . "It was Nelson's idea."

The reality is that we will perhaps never get it right in anybody's eyes. I certainly don't want to stand in front of you and speak at you once a month. I do, however, have to get things done, drive agendas, and ensure productivity. It's all about balance. We have to balance what everybody wants, honor diverse ideas, and find ways to all feel better about the outcomes.

The length of this memo, the risk involved in writing it, and spirit in which it is being sent should indicate my commitment to help us get to a better place. This is all about trust. I trust that you will respond in kind and help move us toward GREATNESS!

A final thought—Am I wrong to assume that we should be able to model what we expect our students to do? If I am, change the title of this memo to: He's Finally Lost It!

* * *

I read this memo to two members of my leadership team before sending it. I also shared it with another staff member who had never had a conversation with me about faculty meetings. They all seemed shocked that I had written it, but concurred that I should send it out. The memo went out on a Friday around noon.

As I was preparing to leave for the weekend, I received a phone call from a part-time teacher who had read the memo at home. She called to thank me for having the courage to tackle this issue. She went on to say that she had always been surprised at how people acted at our meetings. She sounded emotional as she praised the accuracy of my words. Several minutes later another staff member dropped into my office and relayed a similar sentiment. I had certainly touched a nerve with these two people.

When I returned to work on Monday morning, I had a couple of dozen e-mails, cards, or notes from members of my faculty. Nearly all of them were complimentary about the memo. Most of the teachers agreed that the call for addressing our professionalism in meetings was justified. Some of the communications included admissions of guilt and promises of better work in the future. Only a few of the staff members appeared defensive and tried to make excuses for their contributions to the problem or denied that a problem existed.

Although I had broken my rule about lecturing to the entire group, it was clearly the right thing to do. I had publicly validated what most of our faculty had become frustrated with. This was a case of doing the wrong thing for the right reasons. The following three e-mails that I received in response to my courageous memo illustrate just how right it was.

* * *

Just a quick response to your memo to all staff. Since your arrival faculty meetings have become interesting (sometimes even exciting), informative, and stimulating. I was talking just the other night about how dramatically the overall climate has changed here. You are extremely supportive of STUDENTS & STAFF. PLEASE DO NOT CHANGE your methodology or your style in any way. I sincerely believe that a VAST MAJORITY of staff (and students as well) absolutely support most everything that is happening. It would be a very small minority that may NOT LIKE CHANGE, or RESIST any NEW IDEAS. PLEASE "stay the course." We celebrate and need your leadership here! You are much appreciated!

* * *

Good memo, Nelson. I will take the part that is mine and try to improve the weak areas. It was a brave and probably needed missive. The best faculty meeting for me personally would include information, reasonable discussion, and an opportunity for me to hear what your expectations as my administrator are. Probably old school, but there I am. I'm truly horrified that your little presentations caused "jealousy and strife." What is that about? Maybe we are just slipping into bad habits here and need to be shaped up a bit. Thanks for your honesty—I would never doubt your integrity in the slightest.

* * *

Regarding your memo, all I can say is "Right On." As I think I wrote you about this time two years ago, the sea of change that has come about—and continues to evolve—because of your leadership never ceases to amaze me. For the first time in over three decades here, I come to school certain of the direction in which we should all be headed, and satisfied that the person in charge of herding us, as a group of cats, does it with grace, humor, and great competence. Your sincere interest in the greater good of the school, the welfare of the kids, and your interest in the needs and direction of the staff is unceasing, and that shows in all that we have done here. I find the faculty meetings refreshing, valuable, frustrating, and challenging—all at the same time. That is good, I think. Nothing is going to be perfect, and though I sometimes marvel at your patience in the midst of the arena, I feel that generally most leave the meetings feeling that something truly good is happening here.

Try to keep in mind that you are still performing amazing miracles, and, slowly, the great ship is turning, sometimes against its own wake. It will take a while yet, and some may have to decide to jump off if they can't take the life preservers that you continually throw out. That is just the way it is. Keep up the good work.

* * *

Based on this and other feedback, the risky memo appears to have accomplished something positive. Our faculty meetings still have room for improvement, but at least the issues have been clearly defined. Because the memo was written with the best teachers in mind, breaking the rule—at least in this instance—was the right thing to do.

Lost in Translation
Make an Effort to Make Others Comfortable

Something that I may never get used to is the reality that I have positional power. There is not a cell in my body that works on the idea that the title of Principal should be a source of intimidation. I am often reminded, however, that what I would like to project is often lost in translation. Parents call to discuss a meeting that I had with their son or daughter and indicate that the student was unable to express himself or herself because I am the principal. I recall the same meeting and say to myself, "No way! What planet are they on?" I work so hard to make students feel at ease. I wonder if the parents are projecting their past experiences with principals on their children.

The same situation occurs with teachers. I have sent word to teachers asking them to stop by and see me for a few minutes about something quite insignificant, only to discover that I elevated their anxiety because they were being summoned to my office. On one occasion a staff member actually went to find a union representative to accompany her to the office. These outcomes are so foreign to my way of thinking that I have to really work at dispelling the myth of power that is associated with my position.

I make a conscious effort not to be positional. I rarely sit at my desk during meetings in my office. Instead, I have a small meeting table set up for that purpose. As the meeting winds down, I usually ask the people I am meeting with to repeat what I said in order to check whether they understood what I said. I often ask them openly if they felt I was a good listener. I cannot imagine what the perceptions of my power rating would be like if I did not do these things. Nevertheless, positional power isn't all bad. At times it can take a funny twist, as noted in the following story.

During Kennebunk's Spirit Week assemblies I have participated in a fundraiser in which the students are allowed to "Suspend the Principal." They buy yard-long strips of duct tape for one dollar a strip. They use the tape to stick me to a wall while I am standing on a stool. Eventually, after they have purchased enough duct tape to securely fasten me to the wall, the stool is removed. I am left suspended there as they exit the assembly. Students get such a kick out of doing this.

I recently bumped into a parent of a student who had graduated two years ago. I had probably talked to this student only five or six times during his high school days, so it was not as if we were closely connected. The parent indicated that she had gone to visit her son at college and thought I might want to know that my picture was hanging in his dorm room. It seemed a bit strange that a sophomore in college would have a picture of his high school principal on his bulletin board. The picture was a newspaper photo of me being suspended during an assembly. I guess that my willingness to be suspended had made quite an impression on that young man.

Another example of the fun that can arise from positional power took place during Spirit Week in my first year at Kennebunk High School. The final activity of our week-long, mid March program is the ever-popular Air Band competition. Each class is judged on a dance routine that they practice and polish throughout the week. The faculty participates as well. Our teachers had selected a disco theme for their Air Band, and I opened the number by doing a few fancy moves with our dance teacher at center court. Those ten or fifteen seconds of twirling the dance teacher around made me an instant hero in the eyes of the students. I guess those disco lessons my wife dragged me to in the 1980s finally paid off. Students came up to me after the assembly and gave me high fives and congratulated me for doing such a great job. It was as if they believed I had practiced for hours just to impress them. In reality I had practiced for three minutes and was just going through the motions without really understanding how important this activity was to our students. Students could not believe that I could dance. After all, I was that man in the principal's office.

The teachers' Air Band routine ended with our snake dancing out of the gymnasium. I brought up the rear of the line carrying a placard that read, "It should be Spirit Week every week." As the snake moved out of the gymnasium, the students gave us a roaring standing ovation. School spirit was alive and well at K.H.S. Students love to see their teachers and administrators having fun and being real. They love seeing our humanity.

Throughout my career in education I have never felt a need to act a certain way in order to sustain the dignity of my position. On Fridays the faculty dresses down. This is an idea we borrowed from the corporate world. We donate one dollar to our faculty scholarship fund, and that is our ticket to wear jeans and a polo shirt for the day. I love Fridays—dressing down gives me a whole new outlook at school. The students think it's cool to see me dressed in something other than a suit and a tie. Many would never think a principal would wear jeans.

Students are much better than people give them credit for when it comes to adapting to situations. They may laugh at me as I am being duct-taped to the wall, cheer as I do some disco moves, or think it is neat that I wear jeans—but they also respond appropriately when I am conducting a dignified graduation activity. When a serious situation occurs, they know who their teachers and administrators are. I have come to believe that these little things that I do really count. They actually contribute to my success. They go a long way toward minimizing the negative impact that positional power can have on my efforts to lead.

3

Giving Students
a Voice

Giving Students a Voice . . . Brilliant

Seek to Inspire Rather Than Control Them

One must leave one's comfort zone in order to accomplish good things in schools. Nowhere is this idea of risk taking for the greater good more clearly demonstrated than in giving students a voice. Giving students a voice is not a simple proposition. The idea carries with it all sorts of anxiety and fear. What appears on the surface to be a fairly natural occurrence is actually a rarity in schools. It requires a tremendous amount of trust from adults, a tremendous amount of responsibility from students, and a framework that provides opportunities for student leadership.

I am not sure where and when my involvement with student voice began. It probably started during my early experiences in coaching when I discovered that I could get a stronger commitment from my players when they had some say in what we were doing. Back then, as now, coaching was essentially a dictatorship with the coach pulling all the strings. I had little success doing that. I slowly discovered that I got better results from my players when I involved them in the process. Their voice in the team's direction appeared to inspire them, whereas my attempts to control everything seemed to diminish their performance.

The transfer of this concept to the classroom and the entire school experience is obvious. In its most basic form, giving students a voice is really giving students a choice. There can be little personal responsibility unless choices are provided. I learned early on as a parent that providing a toddler with choices often led to better outcomes.

An extension of this concept occurs when teachers and school leaders really listen to students and actually involve them in the planning. In a classroom setting students can be given options on how to pursue learning a particular skill or how they might want to be assessed. At the schoolwide level they can be given a role in the decision-making process where their problem-solving skills and ideas are valued. Examples of these roles are depicted in the accompanying stories. These stories suggest that instead of ignoring young people, particularly between the ages of twelve and seventeen, adults should search for ways to involve them. All of this brings us back to the question of trust. It is very uncomfortable for adults to relinquish control. They fear that the students will make undesirable choices and decisions. Results are not as predictable as they would be in a controlled setting. However, my experiences with student voice as a parent, coach, teacher, and school administrator have given me very little to fear. In nearly every situation in which I summoned the courage to give students some control, they succeeded beyond my expectations.

The stories in this section provide examples of how student voice has played out in my work. Collectively, the stories demonstrate that I am quite comfortable in allowing students to make decisions. In fact, that is now the case. I have come to trust that the outcomes are well worth the risks. I am certain that I have also learned from experience about developing frameworks and routines that support quality student voice. So my comfort zone has expanded as I have gained experience. It has become quite natural for me to try to inspire students to lead rather than to impose my leadership on them.

Several days ago while grocery shopping, I ran into a wonderful teacher with whom I once worked. We exchanged pleasantries and spoke for five or six minutes about our respective schools. As we ended the conversation she left me with a comment that best describes the value of student voice. She said that students must be given the opportunity to become involved. She went on to say that without that involvement, students would ultimately have little ownership or sense of belonging in the school. They would be just visitors rather than contributing members.

There lies the power of student voice and why I strive to go beyond my comfort zone to provide opportunities for it to happen. I do not want students to feel like prisoners in our school. I want them to feel like volunteers. A person can make great accomplishments in a voluntary setting. I believe that by listening to students' voices, they in turn become more motivated. Educators should seek to inspire rather than control!

Magical Microwaves
Convince Students That You Will Listen

As part of our Comprehensive School Reform grant at Leavitt Area High School, we replaced our traditional homeroom period with an advisory program. Teachers and staff felt that the homeroom program was not really helping our students. Groups were large and impersonal, and teachers had time for little more than taking attendance and presenting daily announcements. The advisory program held much more promise. It was intended to help faculty and staff personalize our school by getting to know our students well. We felt that a period of daily contact with a group of twelve to thirteen students, in which we focused on academic and personal planning, would reduce the number of students who felt alienated upon graduating from our school. The advisory program had a fairly detailed curriculum, which included the idea that these daily meetings would enable our students to express their thoughts and feelings about school issues. In short, we were saying that advisory was a vehicle that could be used to empower student voices. The concept of student voice had been introduced to students and heavily promoted, but there was little evidence that the students trusted that adults would ever listen to them.

One of our October advisory agendas was to have teachers facilitate a group discussion on school issues. During this twenty-minute activity, I walked around the school peeking into advisory groups. I noticed various levels of compliance with the planned activity. Some groups seemed to be in the midst of a passionate debate over a pertinent topic, whereas others were marginally involved or simply not participating. There were a number of students whose eyes looked glazed, as if to say, "This is such a waste of time. Nothing we say will make a difference."

Later that same day, a teacher was in the main office on routine business, and we struck up a casual conversation. As we drifted to the topic of advisory, he mentioned that his students were really worked-up during their morning meeting. I knew that he had a particularly challenging group, and I nodded in acknowledgment that the activity must have been difficult for him. Eventually we talked about the main concern for this particular group of students. It seemed that they were very frustrated by the lack of student accessibility to a microwave oven during lunch. Some students were able to negotiate the use of an oven through the kitchen staff or a teacher, but for the most part students were not able to count on this convenience every day.

As this conversation continued, I found myself switching my attention away from what the teacher had experienced with his group of frustrated students to the obvious question: Why didn't our students have access to a microwave? In a matter of minutes, the plan of action was clear. I envisioned that the desired outcome was going to have far-reaching implications.

I planned to purchase two microwaves and have them set up in the cafeteria for lunch the next day. The next morning, the teacher was going to tell his advisory group that he had brought their concern to the principal. If asked how I responded, he would indicate that I had been somewhat sympathetic. We, of course, predicted their lack of trust and their feelings that nothing would actually happen. We decided that the teacher would not tell them about the surprise purchase. Upon entering the cafeteria, the students would see two microwave stations set up. We hoped this would begin to dispel the myth that adults never listen to children.

The outcome of our plan was magical. Word of the new microwaves and how they came to be traveled through school faster than a UFO sighting. In the ensuing days and weeks, we saw a significant increase in students using their voices. My daily calendar suddenly became splattered with appointments for students who wanted to be heard relative to one issue or another. Our future school issues discussions appeared to have higher levels of positive participation from the students. Advisors reported that, in general, students were beginning to open up. Eventually our desire to create more student voices became an important part of the school culture. The magical microwaves had certainly served as a catapult for our early progress.

Four years later, when I changed jobs and became principal at Kennebunk High School, part two of the microwave story was written. Two weeks into the school year, I discovered that students did not have access to a microwave oven during lunch. I immediately went to the Student Council and suggested that THEY come up with the idea of creating a microwave station in the cafeteria. You can guess the outcome—small gestures can make a big difference.

If we intend to give students a voice, then we have to be ready to listen. In a nutshell, students have to trust that adults value what they have to say, want to help, and have the ability to take action. It is important to ask what students think, but it is more important to listen to their answers. I have known hundreds of situations in which something good happened for students because they had the courage to share what they needed with a caring adult. Even though I was directly involved in only a small percentage of these instances, they all followed a similar pattern of asking, listening, and acting in a climate of trust.

Elevating Student Voice
A Reform Strategy That Keeps On Giving

The flight from Seattle to Maine might have seemed a lot longer had it not been for the satisfaction I had felt earlier that morning. I had just watched five of my former students dazzle an audience of eighty workshop attendees at the Coalition of Essential Schools' Fall Forum. These were students I had met four years earlier as wide-eyed, apprehensive ninth graders entering Leavitt Area High School in Turner, Maine. Now they were seniors, seizing the opportunity to talk about the impact that their leadership had on their school and to provide prescriptions to school leaders looking for reform models that would make a difference.

Their workshop, entitled "Giving Students Voice and Learning to Listen," featured five programs that generated high interest and thoughtful questions from the audience. The programs, which had all been created during their four years at Leavitt, encompassed student advisories, service learning, a reformed school government, a challenge day program, and peer mediation and civil rights teams. Each student spoke eloquently about how he or she had contributed to the growth of these initiatives. The passion and conviction apparent in their voices overshadowed the details of each program, confirming that this workshop was more about what they had to say than it was about the initiatives they were describing.

Before my plane had completed its taxi to the runway, I congratulated myself for the role I had played in shaping these programs and providing young people with such rich opportunities in leadership. I had already reflected on the possibility for personal growth that these students had been afforded during their high school experience. By the time the plane took off, I was certain that I had made a huge difference in their young lives. I thought about the rush they must have felt as they received a standing ovation following their presentation. The plane floated high above the snow-covered mountains, and I was physically and emotionally on top of the world.

My mind went back to the early beginnings of the programs the students had spoken about. Each of them carried an element of risk that pushed me to the edges of my comfort zone, and each program depended on the emergence of student leadership for success. The workshop was, for me, a celebration of marvelous results.

The solitude of the long flight east allowed further reflection and the realization that what I had given these students paled in comparison to what they had given me. The discovery of student voice had transformed my career as a school leader and defined my 31-year ministry in education. These students, and others like them, had taken the cornerstone of my work, named it, and elevated it. As a result of their passion, resilience, and achievements I have been able to crystallize what I stand for and how it shapes my work. This has boosted my morale, fortified my commitment, and inspired more success as a school administrator.

Student voice is obviously not a new concept. Every educator realizes that the teachers who are held in the highest esteem have a special ability to connect with students; graduates seem to remember best those adults who showed them the greatest respect. Listening, caring, and understanding form the foundation of student–teacher relationships, and these skills are equally applicable to an administrator's work with the entire student body. A school principal who uses this personalized approach can create an effective school where student voice plays a vital role in the organization.

As my flight wore on, some of the hype that had surrounded the day's events began the descent into normalcy. I was saddened that I had probably just shared my last experience with these wonderful students. I had left Leavitt Area High School several months earlier to become principal of Kennebunk High School, and this trip to Seattle with my former students had been an unfinished commitment. I wondered if these five students knew how much of what I had learned from them had been put into motion at my new school. I wondered if they could truly appreciate that the culture of student voice and the student ownership that it produces were already generating positive changes at Kennebunk High School.

Did they know that all schools have similar students with awesome voices waiting for their potential to be tapped? As my plane touched down at Portland's International Jetport, I knew, more than ever, that the concept of giving students a voice was more than jargon. For me, I had discovered a powerful strategy for school reform, and it had become an important element of my work.

The Principal with Two Heads
Get Used to Being Upstaged by Students

The notion of student voice was really taking off at Kennebunk High School when two members of our leadership team came into my office to share some great news. It seemed that the student forum, which they had helped organize several weeks earlier, was on the verge of a major accomplishment. The student forum, comprised of seventy students who each represent an advisory group, meets twice monthly to talk about students' concerns and acts as a communication link between administrators and the student body. At that day's meeting, the forum had reached a decision to sponsor a schoolwide fundraiser to benefit Schenck High School and Stearns High School.

Those high schools were located about 200 miles north of Kennebunk in communities that had recently been devastated by the closing of the Great Northern Paper Mill. I shared my staff members' excitement at the prospect of this student group tackling such a worthwhile project. I immediately asked to be put on the next student forum agenda. I wanted to show my support and enthusiasm for their idea.

The following week, I walked into the student forum meeting with a spring in my step and a smile on my face. As soon as I got the opportunity, I went overboard praising their idea and thoughtfulness. I went on to tell them that I would take whatever money they raised and turn it over to the principals at the respective schools. I would ask them use it to fund a schoolwide assembly. My hyperenthusiasm did not blind me from the disappointment I saw in the faces of the students when I mentioned the plan. The students were staring at me as if I had two heads. One young lady, who had the courage to speak for everyone else in the room, told me that they respectfully thought my idea was foolish. In effect, the students thought that providing a distressed community with some "lame" motivational assembly was the last thing on their minds. Fortunately, I was smart enough not to try to defend my idea. Instead, I opened the meeting for their ideas about what we could do with the money raised. Several students had ideas such as a coat drive or food drive, but none of them seemed to please the group. Eventually, one of the students made a proposal that stuck. She said, "What we originally wanted to do was help these students directly. So why not subsidize the Proms at each of these schools? I think their students would really like that."

The support for her idea was instantaneous. Everyone in the room knew how special the Prom experience can be to a student. Everyone in the room also knew how much better her idea was than the one their principal had proposed.

Several months later, we sent a check for one thousand dollars to each of the two high schools in support of their Proms. Our high school was the subject of numerous newspaper articles, several television news spots, and was even written up in *Downeast* magazine and *Education Today*. The student forum had made a strong initial contribution to our efforts to encourage stronger student participation. And I, the principal with two heads, was reminded once again about the wonder of student voices.

Tripping Over a Gem

Like Midas, the Students Can Have a Golden Touch

One night I was home peacefully watching a Celtics game on the upstairs TV when my wife, Sharon, called me downstairs. She wanted me to see the ending of a program she had been watching on television. I rushed downstairs and caught the last half hour of a show from the Teen Files series from AIMS Multi-Media, produced by Arnold Shapiro, entitled *Surviving High School*. I was intrigued by the content of the show and the explanation Sharon had given me about the scenes I had missed. She felt that I could use this material at Leavitt Area High School to improve school climate. My brief assessment of the program led me to agree with her. The next day, I ordered a tape of the program for the school and started to think about how I could use this show with my students.

The initial idea was to invite fifty student leaders to an evening program. We would show the ninety-minute video, do a few quick discussion activities, and end with a pizza party. At the conclusion of the program, I would get student input about if and how we should use this show with other students in the future. The video was a big hit for the twenty-six students who courageously accepted our invitation. In fact, I was floored by the emotional response they had to the entire program. Our plan, which was simply to get their feedback at the end of the program, went by the wayside. The students had seen something that evening that related to their school and their lives. They were not going to leave until they had a plan to implement it. The projected ending time for the program had been 8:00 PM. Sharon and I finally got the last student to leave at 11:00 PM! I remember sitting in a huge circle on our auditorium stage for several hours. We listened to the students speak passionately about their lives at school. Their voices showed differing points of view about the teen issues they had just been exposed to, but the group shared an intensity of purpose about what they wanted to do next.

Before we wound down that evening, we had created a leadership group that was committed to bringing "Challenge Nite" to each student at our school. They took the rather simplistic program we had presented and expanded it to an appealing student-centered awareness activity that effectively addressed student issues such as bullying, cliques, and suicide. In just one activity, participants would be challenged to change their attitudes and behaviors relative to these topics in order to create new norms for our school.

Over the next year we hosted four Challenge Nites with nearly half of our seven hundred and fifty student body participating. The following summer, this same student leadership group planned the entire freshman orientation day program with a Challenge Nite focus. This idea that Sharon and I stumbled upon had developed a life of its own, and we owed that to the students' input.

I took a job at another high school several weeks before the freshmen orientation program occurred. That was the last Challenge Nite activity at Leavitt. The twenty-six students who had invented the program made a huge contribution to their school. But that is just the beginning of this story.

My new work at Kennebunk High School involved many challenges, not the least of which was the perception that this high school had some serious issues related to bullying. As a new principal, I knew that the community expected me to tackle this problem head on. The advice I received was to increase supervision and tighten up on the rules. Based on my experiences at Leavitt, I decided to take a different approach and instituted Challenge Nites.

Within my first few weeks at Kennebunk, I called a school-wide assembly. I had been told that the eight hundred students would not be able to gather in one setting without being inattentive and disrespectful. I felt if that were the case, then I would discover it firsthand and move from there. It turned out that the students were fine, especially after I addressed the displeasure of senior students who were asked to sit on the floor. My response to their dissatisfaction was an admission that I had assumed they wanted to be at the front of the assembly. I assured them that for future assemblies, I would gladly set up chairs for them. The assembly lasted only twenty minutes, during which I outlined several rule changes that the students liked. Near the end, I announced that on the following Thursday there was going to be a special evening program for the first ninety students who signed up. I explained that the content of the program was a secret. All I could tell them was that if they missed it, they would be jealous of those who attended. I added that pizza would be served and repeated that if they did not sign up, they would wish that they had. This whole idea was a huge risk. A low turnout would certainly hurt our plans to address bullying, not to mention my status as the new principal.

The next five days were a pleasant surprise as students slowly trickled in to the office to sign up. The surprises, however, were just beginning.

The first Challenge Nite at Kennebunk was a huge success. The program struck an emotional nerve with the students and staff members who attended. The video, as usual, brought everyone to tears. More tears followed as students went through the last activity called Crossing the Line. In this activity, all participants stand in a line at one end of the gym and have to walk across the room and back if they have ever experienced what the moderator says. For example, they might be asked if they were ever made fun of because of the way they dressed or looked. Upon reflection, those who had experienced that would walk across the gym, cross the line, and return.

We concluded the formal program with another emotional experience, an open microphone activity. By this time everyone was drained—drained, but far from done. Much like the students attending the late-night marathon at Leavitt, the students at Kennebunk didn't want to leave. I have fond memories of standing in a circle with ten or twelve wide-eyed students just talking. What a great opportunity for a new principal to connect with students.

The next day at school was like a new beginning for our student body. The Challenge Nite participants came to school dressed in fluorescent orange Challenge Nite T-shirts, and the school was plastered with posters encouraging people to be nice to one another. The students who hadn't attended wanted to know all about the program, but the participants were closed mouthed about the details. Universally they said, "It was awesome. All I can tell you is if there is another one, you've got to go! It is unbelievable!"

The seed was planted for a second Challenge Nite two weeks later, and the results were the same. Our local paper, the *York County Coast Star*, helped the cause by publishing a feature article with the headline "Mystery Surrounds K.H.S. Challenge Nites." The students who were interviewed gave the program rave reviews. The town was buzzing about what the new principal had done at the high school. I tried to give the credit to the students at Leavitt, but this program now belonged to Kennebunk.

There was no mystery regarding the changes this program brought to our school. A group of twelve students who participated in the first Challenge Nite went out on their own and conducted a bottle drive in which they raised more than five hundred dollars to subsidize additional nights. They felt that strongly about its value. I received three different awards over the next two years (one from the community and two from the senior class), each citing among my accomplishments the Challenge Nite program. Most important, the bullying at our school disappeared without the addition of new rules or increased supervision. Our school went through dramatic changes during this period. There is no question that many of the changes occurred in the wake of the changes in attitude brought about by this great program. In total, we held four Challenge Nites. We gave this gift to nearly three hundred students before the magic wore off. We now had to find another program that could capture the imagination of our school community as this one did. Perhaps we would trip over another gem someday soon. At least I knew part of the formula for success—involve students in the planning!

As Good As It Gets

Give Students Something That Matters and Watch Them Make a Difference

In service learning experiences, students are exposed to learning that includes the components of student planning, academic integrity, and addressing real community needs. One of the biggest benefits that comes out of these experiences for students is the validation of their self-worth. The knowledge that they are doing something that matters provides students with a sense of value that is hard to replicate in a traditional classroom setting. Service Learning provides students with rich opportunities to make meaningful contributions as they learn about community needs and develop plans to affect those needs. The following is a program that evolved at Kennebunk High School that illustrates this special derivative of student voice.

I had been appointed to co-chair a committee to study the foreign language curriculum in our district. The task of the committee was straightforward. We were to examine our current programs, explore what was happening in other districts, and make a recommendation to our school committee.

It did not take our committee long to determine that our ultimate recommendation to the board would involve the introduction of foreign language instruction at an earlier age. A review of current research and an understanding of state and national trends in foreign language instruction clearly supported this position. Unfortunately, our committee engaged in this work at the same time that an educational funding crisis hit our community. We were faced with going to the school committee with a mandate to increase staffing to facilitate the expansion of foreign language studies during a time when the education budget was being slashed. Our compelling arguments would fall on deaf ears. It mattered not that members of the school committee supported our ideas; the reality was that the district was headed for a reduction in force. Adding staff was not in the cards.

The ill-fated timing forced us to present our recommendations in such a way as to allow the school committee to postpone the need for extra staffing until the budget picture brightened. This is when the idea of service learning entered into the equation. One of the central tenets of service learning is that students are involved in meeting real needs in their community. Well, our foreign language committee identified, or created, a need for foreign language instruction in the elementary grades.

Two other factors played into this scenario. The first was that our high school had included the promotion of service learning in our Comprehensive School Reform grant proposal. We were searching for community partners that would help provide our students with authentic learning opportunities. The idea of older students working with younger students as an avenue for service learning was already popular. Using the elementary schools as community partners made sense.

The second factor was that one of our foreign language teachers was piloting a semester course for fourth-year students entitled "Teaching Foreign Language." This program involved our top language students who visited elementary classrooms to provide introductory foreign language instruction. After they received rave reviews for their efforts and involvement, it was easy to see that these students could perhaps address this unmet community need. They had already demonstrated success on a small scale; it was simply a matter of transforming this pilot program into a formal service learning initiative. Perhaps such an initiative could use our high school students to, in a way, buy the school committee time to fund a foreign language position in the elementary schools. Service learning was coming to the rescue.

This is one of those rare occasions when everybody seems to win. My steering committee was able to stand firm on our conviction that foreign language needed to be offered at an earlier age. We were able to give the school board an option to start this program without allocating any funds—funds that were simply not there. We were able to model for our school committee how service learning works in a very practical way. In the future, this will be a tremendous advantage as our school attempts to get board support for service learning funding. The hope is that the board will have had an opportunity to benefit directly from the program, which in turn may make future funding more likely. Finally, the foreign language teacher wins because this district need has given her pilot course a compelling reason to exist. It goes without saying that the academic benefits to her students are yet another positive outcome. With so many possibilities for success, on so many fronts, we proceeded with a great plan.

I would relieve the foreign language teacher of her normal study hall assignment in order to give her time to plan and oversee the program. She would spend the first semester developing a curriculum for elementary language instruction. She would also develop a cohort of thirteen instructors to match the number of fifth grade classrooms in our district. This cohort would be made up of high school students and include a retired teacher. During the second semester, these trained volunteers would each adopt a fifth grade classroom. They would provide approximately eighteen hours of quality foreign language instruction to students who otherwise would not receive any. If successful, we would continue the program the following year. Should the school budget support the addition of a foreign language instructor in subsequent years, we would simply offer the program to the fourth grade.

How does all of this relate to student voice? The fact that service learning has a strong focus on students as planners of projects certainly applies. Even though, in this plan, the lead teacher is primarily responsible for curriculum development, she has weekly staff meetings at which students are able to offer constructive input. The real benefit to students comes in the form of apprentice citizenship. Our students are looked upon by their young pupils as teachers and role models. The fifth graders buzz with delight as they see their volunteers enter the room. The experience appears to boost high school students' self-esteem and give them a sense of belonging and importance, which are powerful motivations. These volunteers would never consider missing one of their teaching assignments because they believe they are making a difference. In addition, the increased respect that our secondary students are earning from school board members, fifth grade teachers, and the parents of fifth grade students is powerful. Essentially, we place these students in a position where they are needed, valued, and praised.

In a nutshell, this program represents the ultimate in student voice. It demonstrates that young people can make a contribution to the community. The benefits of their contributions ripple out in all directions. The fifth grade students receive a quality exposure to a foreign language. The community sees our high school students in a positive light. The school system receives positive public exposure, which is a vital need in times of tight budgets. The high school service learning program gets a nice boost. And the upper-level language students get an opportunity to participate in one of the most effective ways of learning—teaching others.

Student voice comes in many forms. When it can happen in such a way that it crystallizes the student's value and worth it becomes as good as it gets.

VP and the Suspensions

If You Want Students to Be Responsible, Give Them Responsibility

It always amazes me when I detect discomfort from adults as they hear someone promote the idea of student voice. It is as though they fear that young people will use their voices in a negative way or that our schools are filled with unethical students who would abuse the privilege. I learned long ago that the opposite is true.

Let me take you back twenty years to when I was an assistant principal at Hall-Dale High School in Farmingdale, Maine. Hall-Dale was a typical school that wrestled daily with a small segment of the student body about the issue of tardiness. There were three young ladies in particular whom I found to be a huge challenge in this regard. Nothing I tried had any impact on their punctuality, and the harder I worked to break the cycle, the worse it got. One day, after the routine preaching to these students about the value of arriving on time and after hearing their disdain for our rules, I asked them to join me in writing a new tardiness policy.

I really wasn't serious! I had just run out of compelling arguments, so I threw out the idea knowing that they could care less about serving on a committee with the vice principal. Much to my surprise, they called my bluff and agreed to work with me in rewriting the policy. I didn't know whether to tell them I was just kidding or send out my resumé. These three students were seen by some as less than desirable role models. Nevertheless, I decided to play this idea out.

I would like to claim that I made the decision based on my insight into the wonderful character that these three students kept hidden from the world. In retrospect, I went along because I feared that I would lose any semblance of control over them if I backed out. So we—the vice principal and three of the least likely of students—went to work trying to write a new policy for tardiness. We gathered data from other schools, conducted a student survey, looked at the wording of the old policy, and wrote several drafts of a new policy.

We eventually developed and implemented a new policy, the details of which are not that important. What is important, however, was that the policy was stricter than the one they wanted changed. These students had been given a say in a policy that affected them almost daily, a policy they hated. To everyone's amazement they had looked at it in an unselfish way and acted responsibly.

I so enjoyed working with them (and I think vice versa) that we decided to do an act in the school's variety show. Our act, "VP and the Suspensions," absolutely brought down the house. I rode in on a tricycle as the song "Born To Be Wild" blared over the sound system. The packed house got quite a kick seeing me dressed like Columbo popping a wheelie on my son's tricycle.

When the spotlight shifted to the girls, the roar of the crowd reached an even higher level. They lip-synched to Pink Floyd's song "Brick in the Wall," and it was a riot. We then went through a funny skit that most of the audience didn't hear because they were so busy shouting and cheering at this most unlikely act. To see the assistant principal and three of his most frequent customers on stage together was worth the price of admission.

That evening was probably the closest I will ever come to understanding what a Broadway star experiences. I was bringing joy and laughter to a huge audience, one that comprised many other students who would have to interact with me in the months to come. What the audience didn't know was that the four of us had spent hours together planning and practicing this routine. Those hours allowed me to see the special qualities of these three students, and, conversely, they got to know me as a person rather than a school administrator.

The outcome of this bit of folly was all good. The young ladies' attendance improved; our new policy worked better than the old one; and my relationship with these three previously unreachable students became solid. One of the girls ran for a senior class office the following year and won! Of course, everyone thought that it was a joke and that she would not really help the class, but I knew differently. By reaching out I had learned that if you entrust students with responsibility, they will deliver thoughtfully.

Government by the Students

Create a Laboratory of Democracy

Generalizations are easy to come up with when talking about student government/student council. The norm in the high schools I am familiar with, and I suspect in most schools, is that true student government is practically nonexistent. Schools have student leadership organizations that are given token governance responsibilities. Rarely are they perceived as having much of a say in the decision-making process. These groups usually attend to organizing student activities such as Winter Carnivals, Spirit Weeks, dances, and other social events. These are important parts of the high school experience, but they do not give our young people much exposure to governance.

In most schools, members of the organization are elected. At a few schools students might actually seek election based on some sort of platform of beliefs and promises. Usually the elections are popularity contests. For students, they provide window dressing for their college applications and little in the way of leadership experience. In reality, student government does not provide young people with an authentic laboratory experience in democracy. Could there be a better model? Could there be several?

At Kennebunk High School our student council was fairly typical. All of the popular students survived the election process, oversaw social programming, and occasionally dabbled in some debate about school issues. Some great students were involved; however, their participation tended to deteriorate as the year wore on. These students were superinvolved but often stretched in terms of commitments. When they faced choosing between a drama production or an athletic activity and attending a student council meeting—well, the choice was obvious. The council did not have much power; it was not very active; and the returns rarely matched the investment.

We decided to implement a new plan. There would be no elections. If a student wanted to be on the council, then he or she simply had to show up for meetings on Wednesdays at 7:00 PM.

Everyone who wanted to contribute was welcomed. If students attended three meetings, they became voting members. If they missed three meetings, then they were out on leave. When we started the new plan, we really did not know how it would work, but we ended up pleasantly surprised.

Meetings that used to attract only a handful of the twenty-four elected members suddenly had forty or fifty participants. We had some challenges getting business done with such a large group, but, in general, the outcomes were all good. We had a strong interest and a strong commitment from students who wanted to have a voice. The council continues to attend to some of the traditional social responsibilities that they always have, but students also participate in governance. For example, representatives meet with the principal over breakfast twice a month to discuss school improvement; they provide a student council report to the school board monthly; and our leadership team consults with them on proposed changes and school issues. The picture at Kennebunk is slowly changing. The strongest factor in the process of change is the open membership. That factor coupled with the desire on the part of administration to provide them with authentic leadership opportunities is beginning to work. If you provide youngsters with an opportunity to contribute, they will deliver.

Let me flash back to Leavitt Area High School, where we took a different path as we tried to improve the quality of the student government program. We installed an open session legislative model. In this model the student council wrote bills involving proposed changes in the school. These bills were introduced and discussed in a town meeting format involving the entire student body. Following the debate, the council would either approve the bill or send it back to committee for revisions. Once a bill was passed by the student council, it went before the faculty for approval. The bill then went to the principal and finally to the board if it involved district policy. There were built-in checks and balances with vetoes and overrides that mirrored the legislative process.

This legislative model involved all students in the governance process. Most anyone could draft a bill and convince the council to consider it. Anyone could speak on a particular bill during the open session. Even in a school of seven hundred and fifty students, the town meeting idea worked well. Students treated ideas with respect and listened to varying points of view. Although the concept still needed some tweaking, the objective of creating stronger student voice was definitely being realized.

These are but two ideas that have merit in the quest for providing students with authentic democratic experiences. A strong student council, in conjunction with other student voice initiatives, can and does serve to advance the mission of our schools. The next story about the First Amendment Schools Project takes this idea a bit further.

Thanks, But No Thanks! No Wait! Thank You!

On Becoming a First Amendment School

It was mid winter, February break to be exact. I had driven into a neighboring town to pick up a videotape from the Kids Involved Doing Service (KIDS) consortium. We would be providing training in service learning awareness to a group of district students the following week. The KIDS consortium is Maine's top resource in service learning. I had worked closely with that organization several years earlier. As I entered the office, I was surprised to see the director, Fran Rudolph, there during school vacation week. She, as always, was extremely helpful. She got me the tape I needed and then gave me some bonus materials to help with the student summit I was organizing. We talked about some of the national things that were happening, and we celebrated the fact that one of my former students (now a college sophomore) had just been named vice president of the National Service Learning Organization. That is student voice at its absolute best!

Fran indicated that she had just been talking about my school the other day with one of Maine's Comprehensive School Reform consultants. It seems that there would soon be a grant opportunity for schools to become First Amendment Schools. Both women thought that Kennebunk High School would be a great candidate for this grant because of all that we had done in the area of student voice. I was flattered that they thought of me, and I told Fran that I would consider applying. She indicated that she would forward the request for proposal to my school, and with added encouragement, she noted that she really wanted regional representation in this important project.

Several days later, when I returned to school I started looking at the First Amendment School website and found some parallels between what we were doing at Kennebunk and the mission of the First Amendment Project. I decided to enlist a student to help me sort out whether or not this grant was worth pursuing. The student was the senior editor of our successful school newspaper. Given that the idea of a free press is a big part of the First Amendment, this student, Maggie, seemed to be a logical choice.

Maggie and I went to the website and started filling out surveys that were intended to give us an indication of how well our school was doing with the promotion of First Amendment principles. Both Maggie and I breezed through the survey with little doubt that our school was in very good shape. After about twenty-five minutes, we both, almost simultaneously, put on the brakes. We looked at one another and said, "Let's not do this." It was kind of eerie, but we both had hesitated because of the same question, one regarding whether or not an adult looks at the student newspaper before it goes to print. Upon discussing our reluctance, we both felt that although I do look at the paper prior to printing, my overview is not so much for censorship as it is for quality assurance. We got the impression that this point of view would be frowned upon by the First Amendment School Project, and we got cold feet.

Maggie and I felt that the school had many good things going for it in terms of student voice and student freedoms. We feared that the grant would turn what was already happening, quite naturally, into a crusade. We worried that we might scare people off with a big-time grant. We didn't want to uncover some sleeping issues, such as students making political statements with their dress or unfiltered use of the Internet. Thank you very much, but no thank you. We were not going to apply for the grant.

Fast forward three weeks to a state conference on school reform where I was making a couple of presentations. The keynote speaker was a man named George H. Wood, principal of Federal-Hocking High School in Stewart, Ohio. I was intrigued by his presentation. What piqued my interest was the fact that his school was part of the First Amendment School Project. I made a point of looking him up later that day. I asked him a few general questions about the grant opportunity and specifically talked about our reluctance to apply. In a matter of thirty seconds, he had convinced me that Maggie and I had misread the program's intentions. He indicated that it was a wonderful program and certainly nothing to fear. Thank you very much, I think we might apply after all.

The next day was a Saturday. I drove my top senior scholar to the annual Maine Principals' Association banquet. The two-hour ride left plenty of time for conversation. Eventually I brought up the First Amendment grant to my student passenger, Owen. He was very supportive of our going for the grant and even offered to help me write it. We brainstormed numerous ideas during the long drive. We were so engrossed in conversation that I once again missed my exit and went fifteen miles in the wrong direction.

First thing on Monday morning, I contacted Maggie. I told her about my meeting with Principal Wood and my discussion with Owen. She switched her position of reluctance and offered to help. I met with our Student Forum (a representative assembly with a student from each advisory) later that morning and told them about the grant and how we had come to embrace the idea. Three more senior students—Sarah, Mikaela, and Jared—volunteered to help with the application. The fact that these seniors were eager to help write a grant that would benefit the school after they had graduated was awesome. I think it showed their appreciation for the changes that had occurred at their school over the past few years. They saw the grant as a way to protect the progress we had made and perhaps leave their legacy for future students. We were going to write this grant, thank you very much!

We decided to include three juniors, Savannah, Jessica and Kris, in the process. In this way, we were able to involve the "next generation" should this grant application become successful. We were set to go except for a few minor details. We had exactly fifteen days to complete this ambitious application; we had not involved the faculty; and we really didn't have a clue regarding what we were going to write in the grant.

The first obstacle was the faculty. The students presented the idea at a faculty meeting. The faculty gave the idea a thumbs up, but there was not a great deal of clarity about what this would all mean. A few teachers were fearful that another grant would create more work. The majority of our staff members supported the students, even though it was kind of a blind trust. It should be noted that we had not discussed this idea previously, and the students were not very clear about their plans. The faculty relaxed a bit the next day after they had an opportunity to visit the website and better understand the concept of a First Amendment School. A small minority were, I am sure, relieved to discover that only four schools in the entire nation would receive this grant, thereby making our selection very remote.

Now we were ready to begin writing the grant. We gave the eight students and one teacher the proposal and asked them to bring their ideas to a meeting on Friday. We brainstormed possible answers to the eight major questions that the grant application called for. The team's ideas were quite solid, and eventually we started to see some connections between ideas. Within a couple of hours, we had a skeletal plan of how the grant would be structured. I went home that weekend with sketchy notes but great enthusiasm. After a long weekend of writing, the first draft of the grant was complete. The committee got a copy Monday morning, and they were asked to prepare critiques and suggestions for a Wednesday work session.

On Wednesday we had an incredible meeting. The students were awestruck that their ideas had been crafted into a concise application that was nearly ready for submission. I was amazed at how thoughtful and targeted their critiques and suggestions were. After a couple more hours we had the draft edited and ready for a final copy. The committee came up with some strategies to strengthen our application, and we set a date to wrap things up. We were going to make the deadline, and, more importantly, we were quite proud of our work.

The last thing that we did before mailing out our application was to prepare an executive summary that was read in advisory groups. We encouraged students and staff members who supported our proposal to sign a petition during lunch that we hoped to include in the application. We had more than two hundred and twenty signatures in no time, and the petition became part of our application packet.

This was all pretty good stuff. We had seniors writing a grant for future students. We had students coming up with wonderful ideas. We had two hundred and twenty instantaneous supporters signing a petition after seeing the executive summary. We had an application packet that was really well done. And we had a very compelling idea: We were going to use the First Amendment Project to help our school develop a governance procedure that protected student voice and participatory leadership.

Several newspapers published stories about these students writing a grant. They were quick to point out that with only four schools nationally receiving the grant the chances of success were slim. Yet the student writers indicated during a press conference that whether or not the application was successful, we still had a great plan, one that we would follow regardless of what happened relative to the grant award.

May 17th was the day that the grant recipients would be notified. Kennebunk High School received a call about 9:00 AM. It was a good-news phone call! We had been selected as a recipient of a First Amendment School Project grant. The caller was clearly excited that we were going to become part of their organization. She cited the involvement of students in writing the grant and the petition drive as particularly strong aspects of our application. Because of intense student support, we have the opportunity to take student voice to an even higher level. We have an opportunity to become a laboratory of civic engagement and democratic principles for all of our students. Thank you very much!

4

Educational Change

Start at NO—and Go from There

When No Seems Like the Only Answer, Move Toward Yes with Quality Planning

In my second teaching position, I was fortunate enough (although I didn't know it at the time) to work for a very demanding principal. I was a young teacher with grandiose ideas but lacked the wisdom of experience. Each time I approached this principal with a proposal, he would simply say "no." Being committed and energetic, I would return to him several days later with a slightly more refined submission. During this second round, my boss would engage me in a slightly longer conversation about my idea and then say "no" again. At this point, I would contemplate throwing in the towel as most of my colleagues did when approaching this man. Most of the time, however, I would return for a third discussion with a polished idea and, much to my surprise, the principal would say "yes!" This pattern continued during the six years that I worked at this school.

By the end of my sixth year the initial proposals I brought forward were quite refined, and I had a proven track record of bringing my ideas to fruition. But the initial meeting still ended with a no. It was like we were engaged in a game, but I played it willingly because I knew that ultimately I would get his approval. It is impossible to express how beneficial this exercise was in my development as a school leader. I became very skilled at anticipating problems and planning around them. Nearly twenty-five years later, I still start at no and work from there.

Last year, my school was going through a mid-year review for our Comprehensive School Reform (CSR) grant, and the visiting committee asked to interview several of our parents. I called on a small group that had been regular attendees at our monthly parent forums.

As the interview started, one of the parents began praising the work that we had done to improve the school. She indicated that the atmosphere had changed dramatically and that everyone could sense that the school was totally different from what it had been only a year earlier. Another parent chimed in saying, "In the past, the operative word was *no*. Now we seem to start at no and work from there." I am positive this parent had never heard me use that phrase, but those words resonated in my head, causing me to flash back to my earlier career experiences.

I could recall hundreds of stories describing how many times I have experienced the urge to say "no," yet mustered up the courage to get beyond it. Instead, I will offer only a few symbolic examples that illustrate that the barriers to change are rooted in the simple two-letter word *no*.

* * *

In the mid 1980s, I was working as an assistant principal at Hall-Dale High School. A small group of my staff had attended a summer humanities retreat. When they returned, they were enthusiastic and ready to develop a thematic unit that would involve the entire school. The roadblocks were numerous as they started formulating a plan. Among these roadblocks was the principal, who sometimes resisted change and opted to keep the school in a comfort zone. In addition, we had many staff members, including myself, who had not attended the retreat, and we worried about the level of commitment others would be willing to make. Above all else, the issue of time to do the work loomed on the horizon. How could we ask people to do more when their plates were already full? What could make this different from other failed initiatives in a culture where change was so difficult?

Excuse the cliché, but we decided to go outside the box and approach this project in a totally different way. We had an after-school party at my home billed as a gathering of teachers who were meeting to discuss an exciting new program. Our thinking was that if we could get people out of their familiar school surroundings and into a relaxing and inviting space, their minds would be open to new ideas. We also believed that if we could generate a strong base of teacher support, the principal would be more apt to give his approval. And, finally, if this project could be framed as a special activity outside of the normal operations of the school, we hoped that we could get the type of commitment that was vital to our success.

The outcome of our plan was positive. We had created enthusiasm among the teachers to do something different for our school. Most important, we had put together a compelling proposal that the principal eventually supported.

* * *

At Orono High School a group of staff members worked with me to create an all-day career awareness workshop for our student body. In and of itself, this idea was neither new nor particularly creative. In fact, we originally planned to hold a typical career day where thirty or forty people from the community would come in and share their vocations with small groups of students. Somewhere in the planning process a committee member suggested that we administer the Holland Code Inventory* to students, which would help them discover their work personalities. Before we knew what happened, this idea had blossomed into a major production.

Our committee was made up of many forward thinkers, and they were soon structuring the entire experience around the Holland Code Inventory. We would develop four simulated work environments that would match the outcomes of the Inventory and have students visit and reflect on that environment. Students would then attend a scheduling activity where they would select three career presentations to attend, and at least two of these presentations had to match their Inventory results. If this process sounds complicated, that's because it was! However, we worked through all of the apprehension and succeeded in bringing this innovative activity to our school. The person who originally suggested the idea of giving the students an Inventory could easily have been dismissed. It certainly would have been easier to say no. Instead, other people took her idea,

---

*Holland, J. (1985). *Making vocational choices*, 2nd. ed. Orlando, FL: Psychological Assessment Resources.

embellished it, and created a more meaningful program for the students.

* * *

As I was conducting a faculty meeting, two of the agenda items led me to comment to the entire faculty that it would be so much easier to say no to these items. I explained that I had decided to approve these ideas, knowing they were potentially contentious, because it was the right thing to do for our students—even if it meant some challenges for us.

The first item involved a group of presenters coming into English classes to give our students information on fostering positive relationships. They were going to talk about relationship abuse, date rape, and other related topics. Seen by many as not part of our school's responsibility, this topic was of particular importance to our students. A few weeks earlier some of our students had been involved in an outrageous party in the community, and rumors had run rampant throughout the school. A group of students who were gathering weekly as part of a Young Women's Lives support group invited me to a meeting where they pleaded that the school do something to sort out this mess. Even parents called to express their concern about the rumors and asked if the school could do something to frame all of this for our students. Considering all that could go wrong with these controversial topics, we could have offered plenty of excuses to not do anything. Instead, we chose to say yes, and the presentations went off without a hitch. There was little negative feedback and an abundance of compliments for our efforts. Our students were extremely respectful of the presenters and the topic. We displayed courage by seizing the opportunity to give our students the power of knowledge.

The second item at the faculty meeting was an announcement that I had given our Civil Rights Team permission to put on the theater production *The Laromie Project*. This project involved many of the same challenges and risks as those of the relationship presentations—with a few added twists. The Civil Rights Team members were not experienced in theater, and this was a difficult play. As a school, we had not covered the topic of hate crimes based on sexual orientation. Given the controversial subject matter, there was a risk that this production might become more trouble than it was worth. The fact that we had some good results a year earlier when one of our theater classes had presented the play *Bang, Bang, You're Dead* influenced our decision. That play, which dealt with school violence, had controversial material as well. We felt we could safeguard against all the potential problems and decided to go forward. There was obviously some hesitation in my "yes," but with thoughtful refinement we would be okay. Sometimes the best outcomes occur in the shadows of risk.

When Given Lemons . . .

It Is All About Your Attitude

Change is hard enough when you plan for it and create it based on a compelling need. Sometimes change can be thrust upon you, leaving you no choice other than to move with it. Such was the case at Kennebunk High School during the spring of 2002. I had been at the school for a little more than six months when the reality of a difficult change presented itself.

During the previous six months I, the staff, and the students had instituted a number of changes. Change was becoming part of the culture, part of our efforts to make the school better for our students. We were so busy working at various innovations that we didn't notice that the calendar was approaching February. That was the time of year that the new middle school was scheduled to open. The opening of this new facility was going to leave the old middle school complex, which was connected to the high school, vacant. Because we were drastically over-crowded, we needed to occupy that space.

As the middle school community started buzzing about their exciting move, a lack of enthusiasm among high school staff and students began to emerge. There was an underlying belief that the newly built facility should have been a high school, not a middle school. Wasn't the high school supposed to be the flagship of the district? Our facility was in poor condition. Communities all around us were building thirty-million dollar high schools. Ours was an embarrassment. To add insult to injury, the middle school complex that was being vacated was in worse condition than the high school. There had been long-standing issues with leaky roofs, poor air quality, and substandard classrooms. No wonder that no planning had been given to this pending move. It was simply not appealing, so everyone had ignored it—at least until mid January.

At that time the reality that a new high school was not going to magically appear settled in. So too did the mandate from the central office that we had to begin using that space as soon as possible. It was obvious that there was no use fighting the move. It was time for me to divert my attention from the exciting programmatic changes that we were making to devote some energy to the move.

It did not take me long to discover what we were up against. Staff members' resentment, concerns about air quality, and the inadequacy of the space were just the tip of the iceberg. We had twenty-year veterans who would have to leave their classrooms for less desirable spaces. Change of habitat is difficult enough even if you upscale. A visit to the complex after the middle school had moved convinced me that we were not improving the neighborhood.

We had another major concern. When the middle school annex was added to the high school in the 1940s, it had been purposely designed so that there would be little or no interaction between the two schools. Even though there was no flow with the high school building, we were now asked to blend it into our complex. We were facing some difficult challenges, but we had no choice but to proceed.

When I wrote a lengthy memo to staff about the pending move, I am not sure what moved me to call the endeavor "Project Lemonade." The name became a symbol of how we were going to approach this daunting task. I made no bones about the fact that we were being handed a sack of lemons. I constantly validated my staff members' concerns about air quality, the state of disrepair, and the fact that we were acquiring less than desirable spaces. At the same time, I kept reassuring staff that these issues were going to be addressed. I promised them that we would test the air quality, paint and carpet all of the rooms, and put in new ceilings before they moved in. In a way, I made the community feel sorry for us and our lemons and then got them to deliver some sugar in order to make lemonade.

This strategy worked well, and our staff were able to overcome their bitterness and doubt. The move progressed slowly but surely with little contention. I made a significant effort to continually reinforce some of the gains that this move was going to provide our school. The following list is an example of some of the gains we were going to realize:

1. All teachers would have their own room. This would end the practice of seven or eight teachers roving from room to room.
2. We would organize all departments in clusters. This idea was perhaps antiquated, but it was a vast improvement on the disjointed organization under which we were currently operating.
3. We would go to the voters with a $500,000 bond to renovate some of our space. With the money we would create a visual arts cluster of four rooms and a complete guidance suite. Both programs would stand to gain a great deal from the move.
4. We would carve out spaces for special programs such as Gifted and Talented, English as a Second Language, and Speech.
5. We would move classes out of the basement level of our school, which had been deemed unsafe by local and state officials.
6. By tripling the space for our special education programs, we would alleviate some American Disabilities Act violations.

With the exception of the foreign language department, which was forced to use portable classrooms, all of our programs ended up a bit better because of the move.

At graduation that spring the school committee gave the annual district service award to my staff. They cited the success of Project Lemonade as a tremendous accomplishment. It was exactly that—a tremendous accomplishment. We had taken a forced change, a very distasteful one, and turned it into something positive. When given lemons, make lemonade!

Leverage Points

Find a Common Thread Among a Wide
and Varied Range of Priorities

Education is not an easy profession. The list of tasks never seems to get shorter. Whether it be state or federal mandates, some demanding special interest group, or a compelling change that you are committed to—it never ends. I certainly feel that way, and I am in a position of leadership. I often have to remind myself that those who comprise my staff must feel the same way.

I was in my third year at Leavitt Area High School when the level of frustration and skepticism about our change initiatives reached fever pitch. We were concluding the first year of a Comprehensive School Reform Demonstration (CSRD) grant. Our year had been filled with new programs and reforms that had provided us with a long to-do list. Faculty members were on the brink of mutiny. In the eyes of most, we were simply doing too much. The cry for action was loud and clear: "We need to pick two or three things and do them well. Enough, already, with these ten priorities!"

My leadership team started looking at how we were going to deal with this growing discontent. In our hearts we understood faculty members' frustrations and even shared them. Our intent was to drop back and regroup as we looked toward planning our second year of CSRD work. We were going to give the faculty what they wanted. We were going to reduce our long list of priorities to a workable few.

The process started with leadership team members looking at the eight belief statements that had been the foundation of our original grant application. These were more than belief statements. They were goals that we had pulled out of our school vision. Our task was to rate each of these statements individually on a ten-point scale relative to their importance. We were then going to collate the results, determine the most significant, and take the least important items off our plates. We forged ahead with this well-intentioned plan, assuring staff that we were going to address their concerns. We were going to reduce our priorities. This promise, however, ended up being one we could not keep!

To better visualize what happened, it is important to get an idea of what the belief statements were.

1. Learning is our central purpose.
2. We have a climate of respect.
3. We need to improve assessment practices
4. We need to be confident about graduation standards.
5. We need to involve parents in the school.
6. Students need to take responsibility for their learning.
7. Our school needs to move toward personalization.
8. We have to create a democratic forum for student voice.

The outcome of our individual ratings of these eight statements revealed an obvious dilemma. Each statement, rated on its own, was seen as essential. Beyond that, all of the statements seemed intertwined. Success in one area would strengthen another. The rating exercise showed us that we indeed could not take anything off our plates. All of the items were important. The faculty would simply have to make do.

As we discussed how we were going to share the news of our broken promise to the faculty, a different approach surfaced. Our teachers were concerned about our priorities. We seemed to have too many, and these seemed disjointed. In examining our beliefs, we found that there were strong relationships among the concepts. Our thinking shifted from looking at each initiative as a separate priority to focusing our work on a few things that would have the greatest impact on all eight of our beliefs. The shift in perspective made a huge difference. The faculty diet of things to do shrunk from a dozen items to three.

We concluded that all of our work could be accomplished through three leverage points. First, we would attempt to bring more purpose and substance to our budding advisory program. Although this change involved a lengthy list of things to do, the faculty could see it as one concept. Second, we would institute student-led conferences. This work would allow us to affect five or six of our belief statements because student-led conferences would become a big part of adding substance and purpose to our advisory program. Our leverage points allowed us to address our long list of beliefs because they themselves were interrelated. Third, we would develop personal learning plans for each student. Of course, each plan would be accomplished during advisory and provide a framework for student-led conferences. The focus on assessment and graduation standards would become part of each student's personal plan. As we revisited our list of eight beliefs, we felt that each was going to be affected by our three leverage points.

To some extent this approach was made up of smoke and mirrors. We had just as many things on our plates. The difference was that each item was merely a means to accomplish our goal of working toward the three leverage points. Our faculty felt less overwhelmed. Organizing work around key areas designed to have the greatest effect helps to clarify the connections between initiatives. Articulating those connections helps everyone embrace change and lessens their frustration with lengthy, disjointed priority lists. To this day, I continue to think in terms of leverage points when pursuing change.

Seeds of Mutiny

Recognizing Minority Voices Strengthens the Majority

It usually happens in March, the time between winter and spring breaks when the days are cold, dark, and gloomy—a time when teachers, students, and principals are tired and cranky. That is when, invariably, the ground swell of negativity creeps into our organization. I have been blessed to work in schools with exceptionally high morale, but it is still a rarity to escape March without some breaking of the ranks or the threat of mutiny.

It was nearly five years ago, but I remember it as if it were yesterday. I was sitting in a leadership team meeting listening to my trusted colleagues lament about how awful everyone was feeling. Each member, in turn, shared observations of how fellow staff members were fed up with the work. There were issues of accountability and unmet expectations in nearly everything we were trying to accomplish. We had demanded too much, and people were beginning to unravel. The leadership team was in a panic: something had to be done to save the sinking ship. They feared that we were about to lose all the ground we had gained.

As part of our Comprehensive School Reform grant, we had retained the services of a wonderful school coach. Leavitt Area High School was fortunate to have Ken Nye, an educational leader with great wisdom, as our coach. He happened to be in attendance during this difficult leadership team meeting. Typically, he observed our meetings and offered support and encouragement. Rarely did he give us his personal opinion or try to steer our work. But on that day it was different.

After hearing the members of the leadership team paint the picture of doom and gloom, Ken addressed the group. He said that he wasn't here to tell us what to do, but it sounded as if we were in trouble. He looked at me and said that he felt that I needed to call the faculty together and address the issues at hand. And he suggested that it would be wise to admit our failures, take responsibility for the lack of accountability, and salvage what we could of the changes we had started.

Members of the leadership team seemed to agree with his suggested course of action. As the meeting concluded we were set to have an emergency faculty meeting the next day to address the issues. I was going to take responsibility for the current predicament and attempt to do as much damage control as possible.

The school coach and I stayed and talked after the meeting. He felt bad that we found ourselves in this fix. He apologized for whatever part he had played in failing to predict the current situation. As we talked, we started to generate some excuses for why this negativity might have happened—the cold weather, the long stretch between vacations, the difficulty of change, personal issues encountered by staff, and so on. The lengthy list of excuses led us to some obvious questions: What if this atmosphere was just a symptom of the March doldrums? What if we had only a few disgruntled people and it just seemed like more? Should we really be selling out so soon?

Within about twenty minutes we had selected a different course of action. I would go home and develop a survey to be distributed the next day. The survey would be aimed at really identifying the issues we were facing and attempt to get a true reading of staff morale. Based on the results, we would choose the next steps such as calling an emergency faculty meeting.

The survey went out that next morning. I spent the day tabulating the results as individual surveys came back. By the end of the day the results were conclusive. We found that faculty morale was not at all in jeopardy. The staff was tired, but not on the verge of mutiny as the leadership team had described. There were small pockets of discontent, but for the most part people were on board with our initiatives. What appeared to have happened was that the members of the leadership team had heard the negativity of a few and, being tired themselves, had taken those comments as representative of the entire faculty. The school coach and I had reviewed their reports and assumed the worst. In a twenty-four-hour period I had gone from feeling like a complete failure to believing that we were on a great path.

I quickly published the results and sent them to all staff members. Within the editorial comments, I went overboard acknowledging the hard work we had been doing. I gave voice to those who were frustrated and validated the effects of the time of year, the weather, and other challenges. The cloud of concern for our pending destruction was lifted as people saw the results of the survey.

I called Ken, our coach, and shared the good news. He was pleasantly surprised and thankful that the two of us had processed the situation a bit further before acting. Had we had the emergency meeting as planned, it would have been a terrible mistake. Had we listened to the loudest voices only and assumed they represented the majority, we would have set our work back dramatically. We both acknowledged that perhaps our judgment had been impaired by our own depleted energy levels.

History has a way of repeating itself. Four years later, at Kennebunk High School, I was faced with nearly the same scenario. It was mid March, and the reports of doom and gloom where coming to me from all directions. I sensed, no, actually I knew, that we were not in a crisis.

During a workshop day, I planned a special activity aimed at getting to the bottom of the concerns that were surfacing. I gave each teacher two different colored index cards. I asked each one to write the most positive thing about working at Kennebunk on the pink card. On the orange card, each teacher was to indicate what he or she was most frustrated about. I then sent the faculty to do group work for an hour and a half.

During their absence, I took the cards and taped them to the wall in categories. Seven or eight teachers had said that their most positive experience was working with our great students, so that became a category. A dozen others felt that working with wonderful colleagues was the most positive thing. I taped these positive comments from the midpoint of the wall going from left to right. The categories that had the most responses were closest to the midpoint. A lone response would be found at the extreme right on the wall.

I did the same for areas of frustration, except they went from the midpoint of the wall in a right to left direction. Clustered closest to the midpoint were index cards that indicated a frustration with how hard we were working. Of interest, most of these cards had qualifying statements attached to the frustrations. Comments included such statements as "But I knew this would be hard work," "But it is really making a difference for kids," and "It is that time of year." At the outer reaches of the wall were one or two isolated cards that indicated disagreement with our work. The clustering of cards provided a strong visual effect. The majority and minority views were crystal clear.

When the faculty returned to the meeting room they quickly gathered at the wall and studied the consensus graph that I had created with the cards. I did not have to say a whole lot. People were energized by the positive comments, and they renewed their commitment to the organizational goals. As they wandered toward the negative end of the wall, they saw that only a small percentage of people were really in a negative place. The majority found themselves in company with other like-minded positive people.

These two examples illustrate that systemic change leads to high levels of discomfort. People get tired, and they become emotionally drained. When this occurs it erodes their commitment to the cause. Leaders have to find ways to keep all members informed about what the majority views are. A movement toward mutiny occurs one person at a time. If left unchecked or unrecognized, it can grow into a majority opinion. Conversely, if dealt with, the seeds of mutiny can serve to strengthen an organization's resolve. It can diminish the urge to retreat and create the energy needed to stay the course.

The Paper Debate

Use Position Papers to Promote Change

About a decade ago I started a procedure out of necessity that has become an important component of my leadership style. This procedure, the use of position papers, has become a successful strategy for promoting change and a valuable tool for advancing school reform.

During the process of applying for a Comprehensive School Reform grant, we were forced to make quick decisions on complex questions that challenged our faculty's beliefs. A strict timeline did not afford us the luxury of prolonged discussions. As we were writing the grant application, we did not have the time to gather the faculty and debate the issues in question. It thus became necessary to use position papers.

In these position papers I would try to lay out both sides of the argument and then formulate a plan based on the needs of our school. One of the essential ingredients of these papers was that I had to clearly understand both sides of the debate. In order to accomplish this task, I had to seek out, and listen to, those people who stood at opposite poles regarding the issue. In theory, if I could clearly articulate what both sides would bring to the argument, then perhaps the debate could be avoided, and we could spend our valuable time on solutions. If I could validate the feelings and opinions of both sides, then we could reduce the point–counterpoint scenario that usually occurs when discussing difficult change.

When I sent out a position paper to staff, I would invite them to give me feedback and, more importantly, to let me know if I had left out any critical details. They could e-mail me, write in the margins, or see me if they had any concerns. Often, I would ask them to weigh in on whether or not they supported the idea that was being proposed. I would publish these responses with the goal of making sure that everyone knew what the faculty was thinking throughout the process.

When we eventually reached a faculty decision, everyone knew where others stood. Quite often, people knew the score before the votes were counted. All of this was a tremendous amount of work. I had to research the topic, get a read for individual positions, and continuously provide feedback to the faculty. It was work worth doing—position papers did a great deal of good on many fronts.

Positions papers give a voice to the silent majority. Many people act similarly to deer frozen in headlights at faculty meetings. They won't speak regardless of how strongly they feel about something. Through my words in a position paper, I give our faculty members a voice. The papers also serve to silence those who monopolized faculty discussions. Every faculty has a few members who use the forum to filibuster or push their personal agendas. With the strategy of position papers in place, other members of the faculty can address this vocal minority. They can blame the process when trying to address those who try to dominate discussion without risking their personal status. One of the greatest benefits of position papers is that they serve to shield the faculty from hurtful comments. In a heated debate, some comments tend to cut like a knife because emotions can run high. By expressing contrary views on paper, personal attacks can be avoided.

Feelings of fear emerge when most change initiatives are introduced. People panic about what they fear may happen and often don't listen to explanations that might alleviate those fears. I have found that putting facts in writing gets them on the table and helps people work through the fear associated with difficult change.

In summary, position papers get the job done. Issues are examined from all sides; everyone is given an equal voice; and the organization is protected from demoralizing debate. They afford people the opportunity to look at issues in their entirety, minimizing the fear associated with change.

Two position papers that I used at my most recent school led to the resolution of long-standing disagreements among faculty members. Prior to the use of position papers, the same two topics would surface every year. People would get all worked up, invest in their side of the debate, and become increasingly frustrated when the desired changes did not occur.

The position paper I wrote on weighted grades demonstrates how a compromise can be reached. This very emotional topic had been hashed out over and over in our community with no solution. Historically, weighted grades have always been discussed in the context of winners and losers. You either weight grades or you don't. The win–win approach that I took in the position paper seemed like a logical choice in trying to end this long-standing controversy. My motivation for attacking this difficult question really had nothing to do with weighted grades. It had to do with ending the philosophical division that existed in our school community relative to the topic and putting this question to rest once and for all.

* * *

To: All Staff
From: Nelson
Re: Position Paper on Weighted Grades

BRACE YOURSELF . . . the attached position paper deals with a topic that generates strong emotional responses, and it is likely to upset people on both sides of the argument.

From what I can surmise, the question about weighted grades has been an issue that comes up nearly every year and generally leads to a polarized debate and no change.

As I mentioned at an earlier faculty meeting, I would like to propose a change that would create a weighted system for Honors and Advanced Placement courses despite my personal disagreement with such a policy. I support this proposal simply because I have come to believe that many of our most influential constituents (top students, parents, and board members) are seeing this as an important issue, and we would be well served by listening to their voices.

I am looking at this whole question of weighted grades from a benefit versus harm perspective and feel that the proposed system may benefit a few students, please those vested constituents, and not bring harm to anyone else.

After the faculty meeting, a teacher indicated to me that adopting a weighted system despite our philosophical concerns was a refreshing idea, citing that there were "other hills to die on."

Having said all of this, I encourage you to consider the attached proposal and give me feedback. E-mail me with your response: thumbs up, thumbs down, or anything in between. There is a bit of a time crunch here as I have been asked to report to the school board at the January meeting. We do have a faculty meeting this Thursday, and if everyone has had time to reflect on this proposal, we could discuss it then. If that is not possible, we may have to have an emergency meeting so I can finalize a position that reflects the wishes of the faculty prior to the board meeting. Thanks for the time!

Position Paper on Weighted Grades

This position paper is intended to present the positives and negatives around the questions of weighted grades systems and introduce a proposal for faculty approval. For the most part, this proposal represents the work of a subset of the Strategic Planning Committee, which was done last year and received board approval. It also includes some of the work from various other groups that have considered this question over the years. In addition, it includes some of my experiences having dealt with this question in other districts. I am trying to keep us on our toes in this area, rather than finding ourselves back on our heels implementing something we had little say in.

There is a wealth of information, opinion, and research about the topic of weighted grading systems, and this paper does not attempt to cover all of this territory. The following list of pros and cons is intended to provide a snapshot of the controversy surrounding weighted grading systems and in no way should be considered an all-inclusive list.

Reasons for Weighted Systems

- Allows our students to compete for merit scholarships and college placements, which are often based on class rank or GPA, with students from other schools that weigh grades.

- Encourages students to take more rigorous courses without compromising their GPA, which plays an important role in post-secondary options.
- Guards against students opting for less rigorous courses to boost their GPAs and thereby lowering the school's academic expectations.
- Rewards students for accepting the challenges of harder work.
- Helps colleges see the rigor of our curriculum.

Reasons Against Weighed Grades

- Grading systems are generally flawed. Why would we want to attach more weight to an imperfect system?
- Some claim that college admissions officials disregard weighted grades when comparing students for admission.
- Encourages elitism and disregards the fact that students who can take these courses are tracked to do so.
- Devalues learning in courses that are not weighed and places too much emphasis on the grades (keeping score).
- Contributes to grade inflation.

Qualifiers Regarding Pros and Cons

- There is no proof of any consistency in how college admissions offices utilize the information they receive. For every claim that is made that class rank is critical, there is evidence that students get accepted from schools that do not report GPA or class standing.
- The growing Standards movement is going to change the landscape of college acceptance, with portfolios, alternative assessment, and other factors wedging their way into the places historically reserved for GPAs and SAT scores.
- How can we hope to compare an "A" from an algebra teacher at K.H.S. to a similar grade from a teacher at another high school when we cannot even say that an "A" has some equality between teachers in our own school?

♦ High schools should place more emphasis on college completion than on college attainment.

The Need for a Balanced Approach

Given the obvious disagreement regarding the wisdom, need, and benefits of weighted grades, the following proposal tries to accomplish four things.

1. Attempts to develop a system where our graduates are portrayed in the best possible light as they compete for college admission and merit scholarships.

2. Insures that we are not recognizing fewer students for academic success. In other words, we do not want weighted grades to cause anyone any harm.

3. Pays particular attention to not devaluing other learning opportunities that currently exist at K.H.S.

4. Requires little or no change to current practices at K.H.S. other than in developing the transcript that is sent to colleges and universities.

Weighted Grade Proposal

1. Eliminate letter grades in favor of a numerical system (based on 100). The same grading scale would be used by all, with a 70 being a passing grade and 93 being considered an A⁻. This system should not have an adverse affect on the teaching staff, for they simply would not have to translate a numerical grade to a letter grade, essentially removing an additional calculation when posting grades. It would, however, benefit our students who currently may be penalized by averaging at 94 as opposed to a 93 (both recorded as A⁻) in their GPA. Although it could be argued that the student with a 93 could be hurt under this system, the fairness of giving students what they earn seems more important.

2. Set up a new system for calculating GPA. We currently start with an A⁺ as a 4.00 when figuring GPA and work from there. Other schools send out transcripts starting with a straight A as the 4.00, which puts our students at a

disadvantage. Some schools report their GPA as a straight numerical grade based on 100. We are currently exploring the possibility of changing to that system, which on the surface appears clean and to the point and compares apples to apples. Although we are not yet sure whether we are going to recommend going to a numerical GPA or simply adjusting how we arrive at a standard GPA, a change is clearly needed to represent our students in the best possible light.

3. Assign a weighted value to all Honors and Advanced Placement courses for transcript reporting purposes only. Grades assigned for K.H.S. purposes (honor roll, report cards, eligibility, and graduation honors) would keep the current system. For the transcript, the numeric grade in Honors and AP courses would be multiplied by 80%, and 22 points would be added. Therefore, a grade of 100 would become a 102 for determining weighted GPA and class rank (100 × 80% = 80 + 22 = 102). A grade of 80 would be factored as an 86 (80 × 80% = 64 + 22 = 86), while a 70 would become a 78 (70 × 80% = 56 + 22 = 78). This proposal supports the notion that weighted grades might help our students as they compete for college admission and merit scholarships, but it does not affect life within the walls of K.H.S.

This compromise is fair because it does not devalue the work of all of our students or the courses that they take, but does recognize that they must also compete with students outside our school. I suppose it is possible for a student to become valedictorian without having taken an honors course, but history tells us that this never happens and that concern about it at this time would be counterproductive. The formula outlined (numerical grade × 80% + 22) supports the idea that weighted grades should encourage students to risk taking higher level courses. The student who aces an AP class sees little benefit, yet the student who gets a B gains a bit more. Finally, the rationale behind weighting Honors and AP classes the same is that there is not really much of a difference in rigor across the board. AP courses also offer the additional incentive of college credit based on exam scores.

4. Grades will be reported on transcripts in both the weighted and nonweighted format. Colleges will be able to see a student's weighted and nonweighted GPA and class rank. This should put to rest the arguments that nonweighted grades put our students at a disadvantage and the counter point that colleges do not look at weighted grades (they will be provided with both).

5. This program would go into effect beginning in September of 2002. Honors and AP courses taken prior to that date would not be weighted. The change would be communicated in the Program of Studies and carefully delineated on college transcripts. Going back in time would create an issue of fairness. Changing grading methods for courses that students did not know would be weighted when they signed up for them would create an injustice. It would be equally wrong to hold off on this proposal and start it only with the incoming freshmen class. This would be a tough pill for advocates of weighted grades to swallow. The spirit of compromise tells me that in starting it with next year, seniors will see very little benefit, but each year the impact will increase.

Final Thoughts

It was stated at the outset that this proposal will have little effect on the teachers at K.H.S. For the most part things will remain as they are, except for numerical grades. The burden of this proposal rests with the guidance department and the technology they must use to update the reporting process. Yet according to the guidance counselors, we will be able to meet this challenge.

There are, however, two remaining concerns that exist regardless of whether or not we do weighted grades. We must continue our work in ensuring that these courses are academically rigorous, and we must continue to develop fair prerequisites for these courses and methods of recommending student participation.

Thanks for reading this proposal so soon after a well-deserved vacation. I look forward to reading your opinions about this proposal. Please send me an e-mail, or write in the margins and return this proposal to me.

* * *

The most interesting thing about this position paper was that it was the first one that I had used with this particular faculty. When the topic of weighted grades was being discussed, one of our teachers started to speak in support of his side of the argument. This had been the past practice. It was time now to dig into our trenches. He was politely cut off by a colleague who said that anything anyone might want to say about this subject was fairly covered in the position paper. We went right to a vote. In the end, the faculty voted with a strong majority to adopt my proposal. The weighted grade debate no longer surfaces annually, which has certainly lifted faculty morale.

The paper regarding a fixed calendar shows how position papers can be used to make a change in a bad procedure. Any previous discussion regarding changes to a set calendar did not muster a majority. It was obvious to me that we had a bad policy, but any discussion about changing it failed because the vocal minority controlled the debate. The position paper revealed the views of the silent majority, and subsequently the vote to change the procedure was successful. Previous votes had failed because those silent people had no idea that others supported their views. They made the assumption that those who spoke the loudest held the majority view, and they simply went along.

* * *

Position Paper on Fixed Calendar

I propose that we move to a set calendar where blue and white dates are predetermined and remain fixed regardless of school cancellations. In other words, if today is supposed to be a white date and we do not have school, the following day will be a blue day. Four arguments in opposition to this idea follow:

1. Students would not have their materials with them if school was cancelled and consequently would not be prepared for their classes upon returning to school the next day.

2. Teachers who try to keep similar courses offered in different blocks in the same place for ease of planning and preparation would be out of sync.

3. Teachers who plan one day at a time obviously would want to execute the plan they were prepared for on the day of the cancellation.

4. The calendar might become unbalanced if all cancellations fell on a white or blue day.

For each of the above arguments, I believe there are opposing thoughts. In terms of students not having their homework ready, I believe that most students will meet our expectations provided they are clear. Certainly the set calendar does require a bit more flexibility on the part of the teacher, but my experiences tell me that this is not a hard adjustment. In regard to teacher planning, I would think that the number of teachers who have their classes locked in day in and day out are very few.

Similarly, I doubt many teachers work in the "one day at a time" mode. If they did, they would simply end up with a day already planned that they could execute two days after the cancellation.

In terms of creating an imbalance of white and blue days, this has rarely happened. Occasionally, we have had to make a one-day adjustment at the end of the quarter (returning to the set calendar thereafter). More often than not, the imbalances created worked themselves out through other scheduling adjustments, such as when we do testing, assemblies, etc.

The positive arguments for a set calendar all have to do with organizational stability. Any cancellation requires rescheduling speakers, PETs, meetings, assemblies, due dates for assignments, and field trips. This reshuffling not only creates a great deal of work but also creates a sense of disorganization and confusion. The shifting of the calendar also creates a hardship for parents and students relative to appointments in and out of school. The parent who tries to schedule medical appointments during a student's study hall or college visitations around the child's school schedule is dead in the water. Calendars are supposed to be constant, and teaching is supposed to be fluid. I think we are mixing those up.

Although I think going to a set calendar would require some adjustment on the part of teachers and students, I do believe it would be something we could get accustomed to. I do not think the constant disorganization caused by switching the calendar can ever be adjusted to except by realizing that our schedule is sometimes driven by outside events such as Mother Nature.

I know that this topic has been debated in the past and has failed to gain faculty support. For some reason, there are strong feelings, even among teachers who see their students every day, to not change this procedure.

I welcome any response. If there is something I am missing, please let me know. I hope we can vote on this issue at our next faculty meeting.

*   *   *

I have used position papers as a strategy in more than a dozen situations. It is admittedly harder than simply letting the faculty go at an issue in open discussion. The strategy has yet to let me down, so I continue to use it when facing the prospect of difficult change.

Incentives and Resources

Avoiding Gradual Change and
Faculty Frustration

Incentives and resources are critical to the change process. If you try to encourage change without having resources in place, you will frustrate your staff and actually discourage innovation. Without incentives in place, the best you can hope for is gradual change. My experiences in service learning have reinforced the value of these two necessary components in a culture conducive to change.

The starting point of my exposure to service learning began during my first year as principal at Leavitt Area High School. One of my teachers was underscheduled, and I was advised to find something substantial for her to do because the union would see this as an issue of equity. The school where I previously served had just started a community service program that had shown great potential. So I asked this teacher to devote her extra time to replicating this program. Little did I know that this would end up being a great decision.

Luck is always an element of success. In this case, the luck involved the qualities of drive and innovation possessed by the underscheduled teacher. She not only had an impressive community service program running within months, but also successfully wrote a grant that would enable us to begin a service learning program. Service learning is a method of instruction that includes the components of student voice, academic integrity, and addressing a real community need. It expands on the notion of community service by adding the elements of student planning and academic rigor.

This program began out of necessity. Yet allocating staffing resources to a new program had suddenly opened a whole new set of possibilities. The key word here is *resources*. This teacher had the resource of time to initiate a new program and to apply for the grant money that allowed us to support her work.

Four years later, Leavitt Area High School was named a National Service Learning Leader School, an award given to the top service learning schools in the country. What started with an eighty-minute block of time for one teacher to explore new ideas became an institutionalized, districtwide program that was nationally recognized.

Despite the meager resources given to this program at the outset, the funding for the program grew. We were awarded two three-year grants because of this teacher's diligence. The total income from these grants averaged around $14,000 annually. The money connected to our service learning program illustrated for me the power of resources and incentives in promoting change.

We took some of our grant money and established mini incentive grants for teachers to develop service learning activities in their classrooms. The idea behind this was so simple, yet so powerful. Any teacher who successfully created an approved project would receive a thank you card at its conclusion. Inside the card was a crisp $100 bill. This almost laughable incentive was magical. Teachers don't get bonuses; they rarely see $100 bills; and they never get money from the district that isn't taxed or that doesn't require a lot of red tape. They might have done $600 dollars worth of extra work for this $100 reward, but the look on their faces as they opened their cards suggested otherwise. We had found a small incentive that made people want to pursue service learning. I am sure their enthusiasm wasn't inspired by the monetary reward as much as it was by the novelty of having their work validated.

At the same time, we provided teachers with resources to support their ideas. Until I was involved in the service learning initiative, I often had to say no to teachers with innovative ideas. School budgets are developed eight to ten months in advance without the luxury of anticipating what great ideas might come across your desk in the following year. Teachers in most schools are greeted with refusals such as "Sorry, this is a great idea, but there are no funds in the budget to cover it." Is it any wonder why some people say that education does not encourage innovation?

With our service learning grant funds we were able to find the $200 needed for a bus to transport students out into the community. We were able to buy instamatic cameras for a classroom to use on a special project. The removal of the funding barriers made the development of new ideas more realistic. Our grants also allowed us to pay teachers to attend service learning workshops in the summer. We were able to pay them the professional salary they deserved to do this important work. And we had the advantage of getting them to workshops when they could focus on the work, as opposed to meeting after a long day in the classroom.

Another example of incentives for change surfaced during this service learning experience. The first teacher at Leavitt who completed a project reported on her experiences at a faculty meeting. She said that she had never worked so hard on a unit. She was an English teacher who had her class restore and renovate a local boat landing. They had written letters to town officials, kept journals, interviewed citizens, designed and built picnic tables, and so forth. This work was admittedly not in her comfort zone. She concluded her remarks by saying that in spite of the challenging work, she would do it again in a heartbeat! Never had she seen her students so engaged and motivated!

In the business sector change is driven by financial incentives. In education incentives are a bit harder to find. Perhaps this is the reason that educational institutions are so slow to change. We discovered through our work with service learning that student engagement and positive attitudes toward school can be powerful incentives. Whenever I talk to my faculty about a pending change, I am quick to point out how they may benefit from the response of their students.

If, for example, student led conferences could be seen as a vehicle to increase student responsibility, then would teachers be more compelled to do the work needed to develop that practice? I have come to believe that student outcomes are great incentives for change. Outcomes are the profit margins of our work.

Any change imaginable becomes easier with the inclusion of resources and incentives. The reasons for change have to be compelling, and the barriers that make change difficult need to be removed. Leavitt Area High School's journey toward a service learning program illustrates this premise. The notion of incentives and resources—financial or otherwise—can be part of a successful formula for promoting school reform.

A Hard Change

Create a Compelling Case for Embracing a New Protocol

In late September of my second year at Kennebunk High School, I approached the faculty with an eleventh-hour proposal to change how we reported student progress. Progress reports were due to go out four days later, and I felt an urgency to repair a broken system. Despite the odds, I faced the faculty with the following information.

Far and away, most of the parental complaints that I had received the previous year regarded how we reported student progress. Although we did not have a formal schoolwide protocol in place, most teachers reported grades of Ds and Fs to parents. Teachers used several different forms to report this information. All forms were supposed to go to a secretary, who would eventually mail them to parents and send a copy to the guidance department. The outcome of this system clearly showed that parents had every right to complain.

Because there was not a schoolwide form, parents might receive three or four different types of reports in the mail. Some where amazingly detailed, some were lacking everything but the letter grade, and some were simply impossible to decipher. As reports trickled in over the course of several weeks, the lack of a strong organizational procedure caused the school the embarrassment of often sending multiple mailings to a single family. Adding to the discontent among parents was the fact that students who earned a grade of C or above usually received nothing. In our community a grade of C is not seen as stellar work. Finally, and perhaps most importantly, some teachers didn't bother to send out any progress reports.

The change process requires that people see a compelling reason to change before they will consider it. I explained to the teachers that our entire faculty was getting a black eye because of this faulty system. We had many teachers who were working very hard to report student progress, yet the inconsistencies and omissions were negating that work.

I asked the faculty straight out: "Are you ready to try something different, or do you want to continue to look this bad?" I had given them a compelling enough reason, and we got a strong majority to agree to look for a change.

The work was not yet done. We still needed to get agreement as to what we were going to change to. For people to embrace change, they have to understand what is expected of them. I presented a plan that was new to our school, and, incidentally, new to me. As a faculty we refined this plan until we had a consensus.

We decided to print a four-layered carbon copy form of a standard progress report. This form would have eight spaces to match our eight-period block schedule. It would be divided into columns to record course name, teacher signature, numerical grade, and three numbered comments. The faculty brainstormed thirty standard comments that would be used. These were edited and finalized by the end of the next school day. We agreed to use these same comments on our report cards.

We next had to figure out how these progress reports would be completed and mailed. The protocol involved having students report to a special advisory period first thing in the morning. At that time, they would receive their progress report forms. They would take them with them from class to class throughout the day. At the conclusion of the day, they would return to a brief advisory period, and the advisors would collect the forms to be sure that students did not lose them. The process was repeated the next day, as Kennebunk High School runs a two-day alternating block schedule. Teachers in each class would take ten to fifteen minutes of class time to fill in the grade and add three comments for each student. At the conclusion of the second day, the advisors would drop the top copy of the progress report into a labeled envelope for each of their twelve advisees. They would keep a copy of the report for their advisory records and then bring the rest of their material to an office secretary. The secretary would mail the envelopes and provide the guidance department with their copy of the reports.

I have left out some of the finer details, but in general this is what we were supposed to do. We left the faculty meeting agreeing to give this protocol a try. I can't say everyone was thrilled with the timing or convinced that it would work, but we agreed.

Six days later, at the conclusion of the two-designated days, our secretary mailed out progress reports for ninety-eight percent of our student body. All students, regardless of performance, received feedback about their progress, as did their parents.

It was surprising how much the students took to this idea. They seemed to enjoy knowing how they were doing. As a result, assessment was no longer a secret. Most teachers liked the approach because it was actually easier than the old way and they were given class time to do it.

Several weeks later, I polled the faculty about our new process, and none of them wanted to go back to the old way. The change, despite the fact that it was poorly timed, had improved our school, and teachers could see that. Our secretary, who in the past spent weeks managing a failing system, was thrilled with the two-day blitz.

The parents were the real winners. Our school, which had been criticized for not communicating student progress well, was now the recipient of much praise. Compelling reasons make some things worth doing, even if they are hard.

There Is Something Fishy Here

Find Ways to Promote Oganizational Values

My wife, Sharon, returned home from a two-day conference one summer excited about a presentation she had attended having to do with some fish market in Seattle. She said that she saw a video that would be of some interest to me and suggested that it might have the potential of becoming another Challenge Nite program. Could it be that we had tripped over yet another great idea?

A quick visit to the Internet led me to believe that perhaps we had. Pike's Place Fish Market is an open-air market in Seattle that had developed a philosophy for the work place. This philosophy had become the subject of three books entitled *FISH!*, *FISH! Tales*, and *FISH! Sticks*. Charthouse Learning has developed an employee training program[1] from this philosophy that is being implemented all over the world. The FISH! Philosophy is based on four simple principles: play, be there, make their day, and choose your attitude.[2]

I had little difficulty finding relevance for these principles in a school setting. When I arrived at work the next day, I asked the three secretaries to check out the Website. As soon as they did, I knew we were on the verge of something good. It is important to note that these three women exemplify the principles outlined in the FISH! Philosophy.

The secretaries and I talked about the possibility of inventing a program centered on the eighteen-minute video my wife had seen. I mentioned that this could be really magical, similar to our Challenge Nites, and they were with me all the way. We sent out a purchase order for a copy of the video that same day. We were committed to bringing this program to our school. I cautioned the secretaries to keep the whole idea our secret. The surprise factor was going to be important to our success.

---

[1] For more information on FISH! and related books, go to www.charthouse.com or www.hyperionbooks.com.

[2] Lundin, S. C., Paul, H., & Christensen, J. (2000). *FISH! A remarkable way to boost morale and improve results.* New York: Hyperion.

The remaining weeks of the summer were simply dominated by the FISH! program. Each day I would arrive at work and someone would have another fish item for me. My office soon had boxes of fish pins, mobiles, hats, and stickers. Soon to follow were fish tanks, fish posters, and CDs with downloads of songs that we would use in the program.

Amazingly, my assistant principal and the rest of the leadership team never figured out the secret. They knew we were up to something, but they were not quite sure what. The leadership team had agreed to a mystery workshop on our first day back to school. All that they knew was that something sure was fishy. I even got them to agree to a different schedule for the opening of school so that I could do a special program for the students as well. Trust is the cornerstone of our working relationship.

Although the office staff and I were having great fun, we were also going about the serious work of using the FISH! video to develop a meaningful program for our students and staff. I was committed to having a two-and-one-half-hour in-service for all staff on the afternoon of our first official day back. I also wanted to have eighty students participate in the FISH! experience prior to the first day of school. Finally, I was planning to do something relative to FISH! with all eight hundred and sixty students during the first couple of days of classes.

This endeavor was a tremendous risk. What if the idea bombed with the staff? What if none of the kids came for the workshop? What if the student body did not see the relevance of the fish market to their world? We forged ahead despite our fears. I even mustered up the courage to invite our new superintendent to our opening workshop.

As the one hundred and ten staff members walked into the gymnasium on their first day back, they picked up a fish card and were instructed to find the matching circle of chairs. As they entered, the sound system belted out John Fogerty's song "Centerfield" with its chorus of "Are you ready to play today?" After a brief welcome, I asked staff members to make a list of everything about their job that they did not like—things that wore on them or frustrated them. Johnny Paycheck's "Take This Job and

Shove It" and Tennessee Ernie Ford's "Sixteen Tons" played in the background as they completed their lists.

The list-making was followed by a brief report to their groups. A stuffed fish toy was tossed around each circle to designate who would speak. Teachers were then asked to fold their list and place it in a special envelope.

We next had the teachers rate their job satisfaction on a ten-point continuum and place a red dot on a consensus graph posted on the wall. The song "Heigh Ho," from Walt Disney's *Snow White*, played in the background. Most of dots ended up in the seven or eight range, indicating fairly high satisfaction with their work. This was clearly not our typical opening-day activity, and I could sense that everyone was eager to find out what would happen next.

Earlier, I had convinced two science teachers and two math teachers to volunteer for the fish toss. They came to the front of the gymnasium and put on safety goggles, rain slickers, and rubber gloves. While they got into costume, the audience was trained in two methods of applause: the fish out of water clap and the yes cheer. The two science teachers went first with the female member of the team reaching into an ice chest to pull out what they were going to toss.

She grimaced as she hauled out a two-foot long haddock! The audience was certainly paying attention, perhaps celebrating the fact that they were not chosen for this activity. The two teams competed to see who could complete the longest toss as the audience clapped, cheered, and chuckled. The contest ended in a tie. Both teams completed a successful toss spanning the entire length of the tarp we had laid out to protect the floor.

Hindsight tells me that this part of the program actually should have been done after the video had been shown. It was all great fun, but many people didn't understand the connection until they saw fish being tossed in the video. Our volunteers were very successful at completing the fish toss, but their skills paled in comparison to what they were about to see.

We then viewed the *FISH!* video. Throughout the eighteen-minute film, twelve fish mongers toss fish and crabs around and play with their customers, being totally present and choosing to have a positive attitude. They aim to make a difference for people through what they do and how they do it. The fish mongers are interviewed during the video, and they reinforce the principles of play, being there, making someone's day, and choosing your attitude. The video does a great job of selling the idea that these four principles can make a difference in your work and in your life. The staff really seemed to enjoy it. We received numerous requests later to let people take the video home to show it to their families. Among those who made this request was the superintendent!

After the video I had the audience close their eyes as John Lennon's "Imagine" played softly in the background. I asked a teacher who has a great voice to read a series of statements as the music played, statements such as "Imagine if students and teachers were truly present for each other in the classroom;" "Imagine a school where all members choose a lighthearted attitude each day, every day;" and "Imagine working hard but being committed to having fun and playing while you do it." To my amazement, peoples eyes stayed closed throughout the song. They appeared to be making an emotional connection. This was exactly what we were looking for with this activity.

Following the Imagine activity we repeated the consensus graph that they had done earlier. We asked participants to rate what their job satisfaction would be if people in our school were applying the FISH! Philosophy. The musical selection was again Disney's "Heigh-Ho." As we had hoped, there was a significant change in the scores from the first exercise to the second, with everyone feeling much more positive about their work. The dots now were clustered around the number ten—at the top of the continuum. The idea of FISH! seemed to be working!

Participants spent the next hour in group discussions and activities about various parts of the *FISH!* video and how it applied to our school. We had each group design a vanity license plate depicting a quote from one of the fish mongers that they had drawn out of a fish bowl. They also had to come up with a slogan for their group and a song that represented their work. We had music playing throughout this time. All of the songs had a special meaning relative to the desired outcomes for the program.

Near the end of the workshop each group reported on their work and displayed the poster they had created. Among the many positives we saw during this activity was the variety of people who reported for each of the eleven groups. In several cases, individuals who had never spoken in front of the faculty were the spokespeople. It was also gratifying to see some of the most credible staff members enthusiastically bragging about their group's work.

The closing of the program was simply awesome, thanks to some help from a student. Early in the summer, one of our outstanding seniors had come into the office to visit. During our conversation I asked her to help me with this special program I was planning. She had been one of the original Challenge Nite participants and was more than willing to lend a hand. I asked her to take Leanne Womack's song "I Hope You Dance" and develop a PowerPoint presentation with inspiring pictures and the words of the song rolling on the screen.

When the student brought in her work for us to preview, it was clear that she had hit a home run. The secretaries and I were choked up as we watched this inspiring presentation. It was just the ending we had hoped for, one that was emotionally moving and had the principles of the FISH! Philosophy woven in. We, with the help of this dedicated student, had created a great ending to a powerful workshop.

The time had flown by. People filed out of the gymnasium leaving a sealed envelope with their name on it in a fish tank by the door. The envelopes contained their list of things that bothered them about their jobs and a FISH! scorecard on which they had rated how they were currently doing on each of the four principles. We were going to return these envelopes to them twenty-one days later. We asked them to try to live by the FISH! principles during that time span. The next day, in our professional discussion groups, our teachers were asked to reflect on the FISH! program. We asked them to make a commitment to add some component of these new lessons to their daily work.

The student program was held the next evening. We did get eighty students to give up a summer evening to attend. Some leftover magic from our previous Challenge Nites probably helped with the turnout. Reporters were there along with several other principals from our district to observe this event. An extremely positive feature article with great pictures of our students participating was published in the local paper. During the first week of school, we did an abbreviated program for all of our students, which included showing the video and the Power-Point presentation.

So how did this all turn out? The staff unanimously judged the event a great opening day activity. Reflection cards that they filled out indicated that about sixty percent of the participants had really become emotionally committed; the remaining staff were impressed and thankful on an intellectual level. No one indicated that this opening event was not worth doing. Symbols of the FISH! Philosophy started cropping up throughout the school. Everyone could see, hear, and feel that something fishy was going on in this school. The entire organization was affected at some level. Sharon and I had indeed tripped over greatness a second time.

Although this is a story about how we adapted the FISH! Philosophy to our students and staff, it is also a story about finding ways to promote the standards of our organization. The adaptations that we made to FISH! could be made to a variety of other programs. It just requires commitment and courage.

Making Time for Change
Professional Discussion Groups Can Reduce Teacher Isolation

Among the biggest obstacles to change in educational institutions is the lack of time and resources. Even if there are compelling reasons for a change, school faculties are crippled by their inability to find the time necessary to do the work of change. Budget restraints and contract issues make adding time to the teachers' work year next to impossible. Even if time is carved out, it is usually at the beginning or end of the school calendar year. This solution sets up the scenario of cramming the work into several long days—a formula that does not adequately address the reality that sustained change requires sustained effort.

During the spring of 2003, I received approval from the school board to run a one-semester pilot called Late-Start Wednesdays. One year later, I returned to the board and asked them to extend this program for another semester and beyond. Our one-semester experiences with this idea gave us reason to believe that all schools should do this.

The original proposal was born during staff development time in December 2002. Our faculty was discussing the feasibility of accelerating the reform efforts we were involved in based on our Comprehensive School Reform (CSR) grant. We were reflecting on the progress we were making and evaluating how much more could be done.

I remember feeling quite apprehensive about this activity. I saw our faculty stretched to the maximum trying to implement the changes that were already underway. How could we possibly expect people to give more than they already had? My hunches proved to be accurate. Our staff showed strong philosophical support for making more changes, but realistically they couldn't see how this could be done under existing conditions. Our CSR work was already placing demands on them beyond their normal commitments. In their hearts they could see the need for more improvements, but their heads told them that the brakes needed to be applied.

One teacher summed up faculty member's thoughts quite well: "I can understand how these ideas would improve the quality of our school, but I can't see how this can be done without my losing a significant part of my summer or vacation time. As much as I support these changes for our kids, I'm not sure I want to work year round."

The activity ended with my making an assumption that our faculty was willing to move forward, but we had to find a creative way to provide them the time and resources to do the job.

At our next faculty meeting, we reviewed several proposals that would alter our schedule to provide us with more staff development time. Of all the proposals, the one that seemed to generate the most support was to have classes start one and one-half hours later on Wednesdays. By carving three minutes out of each instructional block, omitting a 19-minute advisory period each week, and making a few minor adjustments to our bell schedule, we could structure this time. Our buses would run at the regular time, so there would be no additional costs to the district. We predicted that most of our students would be able to find alternative means of transportation in order to arrive at school at 9:00 AM instead of the normal 7:45 AM start time. Those who couldn't find transportation would be accommodated in various areas of our building such as the library or computer labs under the supervision of educational technicians. Our teaching faculty would be free to work on change initiatives with no student responsibilities for the one and one-half hour block of time.

We had to assure the faculty that this would not be your typical, administratively planned staff development time. I would create the overall framework for our use of late starts to address reform initiatives, but I would not be overly prescriptive. Teachers would be able to structure their work around their individual needs, provided that they were working with colleagues in identified areas of school need. Following much discussion and faculty input, I received a vote of support to present the idea to the school board.

The presentation to the school board was done in the context of the reform efforts that were already underway and our plans for future changes. Late-Start Wednesdays was presented as a pilot program that would enable our teachers to spend more time on change initiatives. I explained that this proposal would not significantly impact instructional time or further strain our budget. The board voted unanimously to support a one semester trial. They did express some concerns about the logistics of student transportation and wanted assurances that our faculty would make meaningful use of the time.

The school board approved the idea because they were very pleased with the changes that had been occurring at the high school, and their vote was a validation of their support for our work. Members of the school board received some criticism from the community for their decision. The perceived loss of instructional time and the perception that teachers already had too much planning time raised questions among some people. We handled these queries by supplying the critics with more information. After weathering a few early phone calls and e-mails, the idea of Late-Start Wednesdays became a much anticipated change for the coming September.

It was encouraging to have the board's show of support. We had just gained thirty hours of staff development time and now wanted to put it to good use. By the third Wednesday in September, it was clear that these late starts were more than just a gift of time for teachers. Students absolutely loved the idea! It became a tremendous morale booster for students and teachers alike. As we worked to find quantitative data to support this program's continuance beyond first semester, we found all types of anecdotal evidence that this was an excellent program.

In early October, we sent out a letter to parents explaining how staff members were utilizing this time and requested parents to give us feedback on how the program was working for them. Over the next month, we received eighty-seven letters and e-mails from parents responding to this question. One communication called our late starts "inappropriate inactivity." Two others gave the program support but needed some additional clarification. The remaining eighty-four responses were letters of positive support. These comments could be broken down into the following general themes:

Response	Number of Respondents
Offered support for late starts because of the great response of our students.	17
Saw it as having stimulated teaching and learning.	13
Felt it was healthy for teenagers to have the extra time.	11
Believed it was having a positive academic impact.	11
Believed it was advantageous academically for students.	10
Simply said it was working well.	8
Thought it was a valuable break in routine.	6
Said that it builds trust and responsibility in our students.	5
Talked about the program being great for the entire family.	3

This program had clearly earned approval from parents. Of course, any time students go home speaking positively about something related to school, the parents will likely follow suit.

The letters not only complimented the school for the late start program, but many letters also conveyed parental satisfaction with other change initiatives occurring at the high school. I am reminded of a quote by Arnold H. Glasgow: "Praise does wonders for our sense of hearing." Our students were going home praising the school because of Late-Start Wednesdays, and the parents were on high alert to other positive things that were happening. It wasn't long ago that the school was the subject of significant criticism.

We also surveyed students. Actually, the Student Council conducted the survey as part of their efforts to provide support for continuing Late-Start Wednesdays. More than eight hundred students completed the survey, with less than a dozen indicating any type of dissatisfaction. Of particular interest to me was a question asking whether or not they looked forward to coming to school. More than seventy percent of students responded that they did. This question was particularly important because twenty months earlier, on another survey, we had asked the same question. At that time, the positive student responses to the question were at a dismal twenty-eight percent. Even if the more favorable responses were colored by their fear of losing late starts, this statistic certainly supported our continuing down the path we were on. A strong argument could be made for the fact that having students look forward to school would have a dramatic affect on learning outcomes.

On the survey, students were asked what they did with their late start time. The range of answers was interesting. The obvious answer of sleeping in headed the list. Many students indicated that they used this time to catch up on their work or to complete projects with learning groups. Some talked about meeting with friends for breakfast; others mentioned that they had formed study groups. At least half of the respondents linked their activities to school-related pursuits. This was another strong indication that Late-Start Wednesdays would eventually have a positive impact on student achievement.

In November, we interviewed one hundred and six students who arrived at the regular time on Wednesdays. Of those students, only forty-two indicated that they were at school early because of transportation issues. The rest came to school early as a personal choice. All but two students were satisfied with the set up we were providing for them during this early morning time.

All of the preceding information clearly shows that this program had won the support of parents and the student body. However, the idea originated in order to help teachers work on change. How was it going for them? The school board would surely be impressed with the view of parents and students, but they would need to see some results from the faculty.

With only twelve Late-Start Wednesdays under our belt, it would be hard to provide definitive proof of improved achievement or to show that our standardized test scores improved. Again, we were only able to provide anecdotal evidence. Over the first dozen Wednesdays, our faculty worked in four different formats. On one Wednesday morning we met as an entire faculty. This was essentially a meeting to clarify expectations for the program and to get feedback on the types of things teachers wanted to work on. Six of our Wednesday mornings were spent in our Communities of Practice (COP) groups. These are interdisciplinary discussion groups comprised of eight teachers each. These meetings had preset topics for discussion and required teacher action. We wanted to implement new strategies in our classrooms. The use of graphic organizers and the development of questions and activities that encourage upper level thinking skills are examples of COP topics that we pursued. Late-Start Wednesdays gave this already successful program in our school a strong shot in the arm. During the previous year, we had required twenty of these one and one-half hour meetings as part of our CSR grant, yet we had not given our faculty much time to do it. Consequently, teachers had to carve out time from their personal lives to fulfill our objective. Late-Start Wednesdays eliminated this stress.

We also spent two Wednesdays working in a department structure. During this time individual departments looked at our reform initiatives from the perspective of their particular disciplines.

The remaining three Late-Start mornings were spent with teachers working in what we called think tanks. These were informal groups who gathered to work on a specific topic of interest to them. A group of teachers might meet to discuss what works with reluctant learners. Another group might work together to refine the use of graphing calculators in the classroom. Still others might want to investigate the Marco Polo educational site online. Brief reflections and reports of think tank activities were collected and archived.

The outcome of all this work is impressive. One of our strongest teachers reported that after twenty years at this school, she was finally getting an opportunity to work on the craft of teaching. Teachers often work in isolation, and we were finally addressing that issue. Another faculty member shared with me how beneficial it was for him to observe other teachers' classrooms. This was the outgrowth of a COP activity on peer support. In other schools, I had tried to get teachers to observe one another with little success. Now it was happening with no administrative mandate. Most teachers simply enjoyed the luxury that this program afforded them to work on things they have always needed to work on. Late-Start Wednesdays helped to negate time constraints. The program encouraged innovation and made reflective teaching a way of life at Kennebunk High School.

I cannot imagine a high school that wouldn't be instantly improved by instituting a Late-Start program or another method of creating professional discussion time. Such a program addresses the isolation that occurs in our profession. All schools should do this.

The Comfort Zone Revisited

A Risk Worth Taking

I am writing the final story of this collection on a chartered bus speeding toward New York City. On the bus with me are thirty-four high school students. They are participating in an exchange program with a high school in Brooklyn. We are heading toward the Big Apple to spend four days with our new friends, whom we had hosted in Maine the previous fall.

We are taking students to the largest city in the United States where they will be responsible for riding subways and buses, with little supervision, throughout the metropolitan area. They will be living with host families representing an ethnic diversity that students from Maine can hardly even imagine. And they will spend a day in a high school five times the size of Kennebunk High School. Am I anywhere near my comfort zone?

Several months earlier, during our annual state principal's conference, I was explaining the particulars of this exchange program with some of my colleagues. My school had exchanged students the previous year with great success, and I was telling my colleagues that we were getting geared up for an encore this year. The responses from the other principals ranged from concern to shock.

"Have you lost your mind?" one asked.

"Why would you do this—isn't your job tough enough?" asked another.

"Aren't the risks enormous? Why would you take on such a headache?" asked a third.

Now, as the bus approaches the city, those same types of questions race through my head. Before we left Maine, I had given the students my five-cent lecture on trust and responsibility. I closed with an emphatic plea: "Be afraid. . . . Be very afraid!" I wanted my students to recognize that they would be stepping into a different world, one that is not anything like Kennebunk, Maine. They would need to be cautious in these strange surroundings. Being afflicted with the notion of teenage indestructibility, the students chuckled about my cautions.

Nevertheless, I hoped that I had made some small impression about their need to be careful.

Thinking back to last year's exchange, I remember a situation that elevated my fears. I was in a huge urban high school wandering around looking for five of my students who were attending classes there. I had lost my copy of the itinerary and did not know when and how we were supposed to connect with the rest of our group. My students were divided among three separate high schools throughout Brooklyn. How was I going to find my way back? What would happen to the group if the principal came up missing?

After one and one-half hours of searching with no sign of my students, panic was starting to set in. Suddenly, I saw one of my students, Kelly, coming down the hall. I rushed up to her and frantically asked if she knew the itinerary. She must have picked up on my stress. She gave me a reassuring hug and said, "Mr. Beaudoin, don't worry—I know where we are going. I'll take care of you!"

Can you picture a seventeen-year-old reassuring the organizer of the trip, the principal, that he was going to be okay? Why in the world was I doing this?

The answer to that question is that I am committed to making a difference. Students participating in exchange programs have much to gain. They will gain an experience that will land somewhere near the top of their most memorable list. They will never forget their exposure to the diversity of New York City. For some it will be their first real interaction with people of another race. They will be guests in the homes of people whose roots stretch to the far reaches of our planet.

Each participant will be emotionally moved by some part of the experience. It may be the thrill of seeing a Broadway show, the awe of walking across the Brooklyn Bridge into Manhattan, or the magnificence of the Metropolitan Museum of Art. Or it may be the sadness and anger that hits them as they visit Ground Zero. Whatever the stimulus, these students will absolutely be moved.

The students will gain an appreciation for city life, a life that is significantly different from that which they are accustomed to in rural Maine. Each student will be changed by this exposure. After getting a taste of the city, some will opt to attend college in an urban setting. Others may realize that what they have in Maine is something they should treasure. All of them will gain a better sense of the world. In exposing them to that wider world, we definitely will have made a difference.

The planning and responsibility associated with organizing such an exchange is enormous. The magnitude of the work challenges every principle of leadership that I use in my work. The assembly of a sound leadership team, thoughtful communication with parents, and the development of trust among stakeholders are all vital components of a successful exchange program. The time and energy put into the details are clearly evident. Just navigating seventy to eighty people—students, hosts, and chaperones—through the city is a daunting challenge. This program provides a pointed example of starting at the word *no* and moving on from there. At every turn in the process there are ample reasons indicating that retreating might be in order. In undertaking such a program, we are definitely leading from outside our comfort zone.

The New York City exchange program is also a great example of the ideal that educators should inspire student voice. Imagine the trust that has to exist for such a venture to go forward. Through this program, we try to achieve tolerance and understanding in a diverse world. We demonstrate that our young people can model that behavior and are able to get beyond superficial differences and speak about changing things for the better. We provide them with a living laboratory of change. And we show them that we value their capabilities. We move them outside of their comfort zone when we challenge them to look at community and global needs.

We end up, then, back at the beginning. Leading from outside your comfort zone is never easy. It involves risk. It can be messy and unnerving. As you go there, a voice inside of your head begs you to retreat to a safer place.

As my bus rolls into the greatest city in the world, my stomach churns with nervousness. The questions my colleagues asked about why I would do such crazy things are still on my mind. Why would I go to the fringes of my comfort zone and beyond?

The answer to those questions can be found in my heart. This program was going to enrich the lives of these students and in some small way touch the world. And I am very COMFORT-ABLE with that!